P9-BHX-580

ECONOMY IN CRISIS

Regional Disparities

The Canadian economy is in trouble — far more trouble than most of us realize. The books in the Economy in Crisis Series tell the economic facts as they've never been told before in straightforward language everyone can understand. Why is unemployment higher than at any time since the Thirties? Why is inflation out of control? Why are Canada's industries so weak? These books explain clearly why we're in this crisis and what our chances are for future prosperity.

Also in this series:

Industry in Decline by Richard Starks
Out of Work by Cy Gonick
Rising Prices by H. Lukin Robinson

Regional Disparities

Why Ontario has so much and
the others can't catch up

Paul Phillips

James Lorimer & Company, Publishers
Toronto 1978

Copyright © 1978 by Paul Phillips. All rights reserved.
No part of this book may be reproduced or transmitted
in any form or by any means, electronic or mechanical,
including photocopying, or by any information storage
or retrieval system, without permission in writing from
the publishers.

ISBN 0-88862-206-6 cloth
    0-88862-207-4 paper

Design: Don Fernley
Cover illustration: Michael Cook

Canadian Cataloguing in Publication Data

Phillips, Paul A., 1938-
  Regional Disparities

(Economy in Crisis)

ISBN 0-88862-207-4 bd.   ISBN 0-88862-206-6 pa.

1. Canada — Economic conditions — 1965-   *
2. Canada — Economic policy. 3. Regional economics. I.
Title. II. Series.

HC115.P45   338.971   C78-001450-2

James Lorimer & Company, Publishers
Egerton Ryerson Memorial Building
35 Britain Street
Toronto, Ontario

Printed and bound in Canada

AUGUSTANA LIBRARY
UNIVERSITY OF ALBERTA

Table of Contents

1
Economic Disparities: The Canadian Reality

There is a crisis in Canadian Confederation, a crisis that won't go away — in spite of all the commissions on national unity, all the money spent on national birthday parties and on biculturalism and bilingualism and all the words written and spoken in defence of Confederation. Since the election of René Lévesque's separatist Parti Québécois, Canadians have been made graphically aware of the seriousness and immediacy of a problem that has been with us for over a century. Regional disparities are not new to Canada, nor are they unique to this country. But in the present situation of a generally depressed economy and uncertain growth prospects, the future for the depressed regions looks much bleaker than in the postwar boom of the fifties and early sixties. If Canada couldn't solve the disparities problem in good economic times, what prospects do we have in the bad?

Despite economic forecasts and federal government programs the problem persists, and there is little evidence of progress toward greater economic equality of income, employment or opportunity. Until the country gets to the roots of the problem, the spectre of national disintegration will remain. Analyzing these roots is what this book is about.

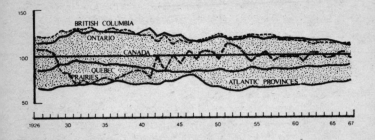

Figure 1-1: Interregional Disparities in Per Capita Income, 1926-1967

All Canadians are aware of the fact that Canada is a regional country. We usually think of six regions: the Atlantic provinces, Quebec, Ontario, the Prairies, British Columbia and the North. Sometimes we reduce that to three: the Atlantic provinces, Central Canada (Ontario and Quebec) and the West — or four if we include the North. The strength of the Quebec independence movement, however, makes it increasingly difficult to consider Ontario and Quebec as a single regional entity. But however we define the regions, we tend to do so on the basis of provincial boundaries.

This, in many ways, is the first mistake in analyzing regionalism in Canada. Northwest Ontario has much more in common with Manitoba and the West than it does with southern Ontario. Northern Ontario and Northern Quebec face many of the same problems as the Northwest Territories, as do Northern Manitoba, Northern Saskatchewan or the whole of Labrador. What we are really talking about when we speak of the have-not regions in Canada is the area of the country reduced to an economic hinterland, supplying the resources and buying the products of the industrially developed heartland of Central Canada. But because our statistics are collected on a provincial basis, it is only possible to measure the degree of disparities by using provincial boundaries. If we could separate the country into hinterland and heartland regions, it is almost certain that the disparities would be even more graphic.

The Economic Council of Canada released a study in 1977, *Living Together*, which documents in considerable detail the extent of Canadian regional disparities. Regardless of the measure used to gauge economic welfare — income per capita, employment or unemployment, or population growth — certain provinces and regions almost always come out at the bottom of the scale, others at the top.

Income Disparities

The most obvious measure of inequality is disparity in incomes. Figure 1-1 shows the persistence of disparities in personal per capita income. This is a measure of income earned from employment, farm income, business income and investment income, plus income received from government transfer payments. These transfer payments include unemployment insurance, family allowances, old age pensions and assistance to the poor. Without these transfers the position of the poorer regions would be much worse. Indeed, the fact that disparities appear to have narrowed, no matter how slightly, in the last 20 years is largely the result of increased transfers to the less well endowed regions. For instance, if we look only at income from employment, farms, business and investment (what the economist calls "market income") on a per capita basis, each person in 1970 in Ontario, the richest province, received more than twice the annual income of each person in Newfoundland, the

poorest province. When government transfer payments
are included, the difference narrows a little: people in
Ontario receive 87 per cent more income than New-
foundlanders. If we look at after-tax income, Ontario's
incomes are still 70 per cent higher than those in Canada's newest island province.

Table 1-1

INDEXES OF PER CAPITA INCOME (1970)

Province	Market Income (Can.=100)	% of Ont.	Market Inc. & gov't. transfers (Can.=100)	% of Ont.	Market Inc., gov't. Ont. transfers, after tax (Can.=100)	% of Ont.
Nfld.	55	46	63	53	68	59
P.E.I.	60	50	67	57	72	62
N.S.	75	62	72	61	79	68
N.B.	68	57	73	62	75	65
Que.	88	73	89	75	90	78
Ont.	120	100	118	100	116	100
Man.	92	77	93	79	94	81
Sask.	70	58	72	61	75	65
Alta.	100	83	99	83	100	86
B.C.	109	91	109	92	109	94
Yukon and N.W.T.	101	84	95	81	93	80
Canada	100	83	100	85	100	86

Thus, even making allowances for transfers and taxes
there are enormous income gaps between the have and
have-not provinces.

The figures on the average income in the North are
somewhat misleading because incomes there are grossly
unequal. The majority of the native people who make up
about 40 per cent of the region's population (over 50 per
cent in N.W.T.), earned less than $4,000 per year in
1970, while the smaller white population averaged in excess of $10,000 per year.

Why are incomes so unequally distributed among Canadian regions? The first and most obvious reason is that wages and salaries paid in the poorer regions are lower than those in the richer regions — and the differences are significant. In 1975, a year when wage differentials narrowed quite substantially, average wages and salaries in Ontario and B.C. still remained about 10 per cent higher than in Quebec, 15 per cent higher than in the Prairies (including Alberta) and 20 per cent higher than in the Maritimes. If we could exclude those people employed by the federal government, those employed on the railways and airlines and those employed by other employers who have national wage scales, the differences in average wages would be magnified.

Employment Disparities

But it is not only the lower level of wages that contributes to lower incomes in the poorer regions. With the exception of the Prairies, the lower wages are compounded by higher rates of unemployment. The tragedy of unemployment is the worst manifestation of the economic distress of the lagging regions. The rate of unemployment in Canada has reached levels not experienced since the Depression. The rates in the poorer regions of the country are even more disturbing. If it were not for the extensive intervention of government in the form of transfer payments, in particular unemployment insurance, and the employment of a large number of people by federal, provincial and local governments, the Canadian economy would be reduced to a level of distress comparable with that of the disastrous thirties.

Even with the present level of government intervention and supports, in the winter of 1977-78, seasonally adjusted unemployment rates in the Atlantic provinces averaged in excess of 12.5 per cent; in B.C., 8.5 per cent, and in Quebec, 11 per cent. Still these figures tell only part of the story. They are regional averages and they are adjusted to take account of seasonal fluctuations in employment. Unadjusted rates are significantly higher in

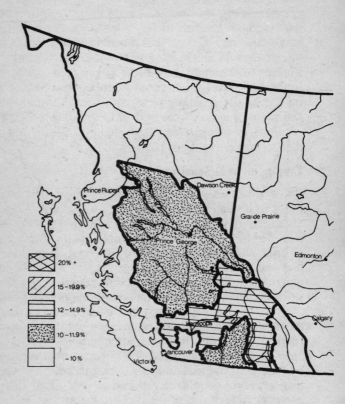

Figure 1-2: Unadjusted Unemployment Rates, March 1978

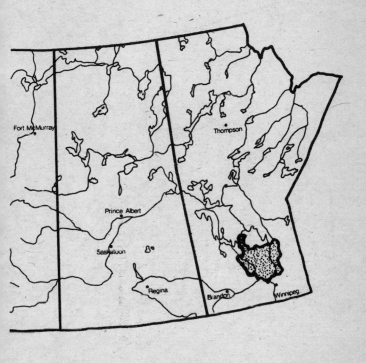

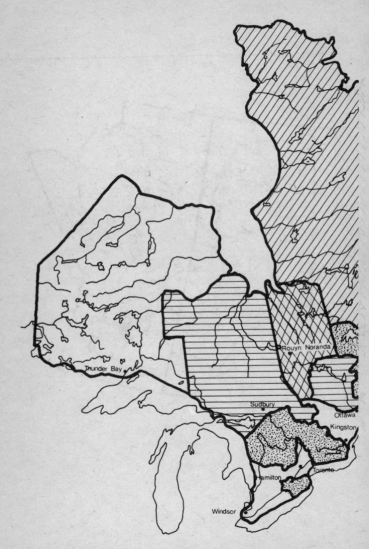

Figure 1-2: Unadjusted Unemployment Rates, March 1978

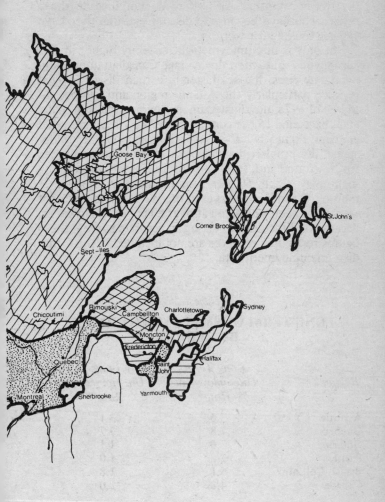

the winter months. Also, they do not include those people who have become so discouraged that they have stopped looking for work.

Not only is unemployment persistently higher in certain regions, but when the average Canadian unemployment rate rises, it rises faster in certain disadvantaged regions, particularly the Atlantic region and Quebec. In March of 1978, unadjusted unemployment rates in many areas exceeded 15 per cent, in some, well in excess of 20 per cent. Figure 1-2 gives some indication of how widespread the problem has become. In some communities (in Newfoundland, for example), the rates of unemployment may reach 50 per cent or more in the winter months. On Indian reserves in the West, unemployment rates have been estimated at over 80 per cent. However, because of difficulties in taking an accurate survey, these figures for Indian reserves are not included in the Canadian unemployment rate.

Table 1-2

LONG TERM UNEMPLOYMENT RATES: BY REGION

Region	Long Term Unemployment Rate*	Very Long Term Unemployment Rate**
Atlantic	7.6	3.1
Quebec	7.8	3.7
Ontario	3.0	1.1
Prairies	2.6	1.0
British Columbia	5.1	1.8
Canada	4.8	2.0

* Percentage of the labour force unemployed more than 14 weeks in 1968.

** Percentage of the labour force unemployed more than 27 weeks in 1968.

In addition to the fact that unemployment rates in the Atlantic and Quebec regions may be a 100 per cent or more higher than in Ontario or the Prairies, the percentage of long term unemployment in the Atlantic and Quebec regions is also much higher. Sylvia Ostry and Mahmood Zaidi in a 1968 study found that the long term unemployment rates in the Atlantic provinces, Quebec and British Columbia stood much higher than the Canadian average. Short term unemployment is serious enough but with the aid of unemployment insurance, workers and their families normally suffer little deprivation, and the worker does not see his or her skills and morale deteriorate. Long term unemployment, on the other hand, is very destructive of workers, their skills and their families.

Another feature of the structure of unemployment, that a high proportion of people under 25 are unemployed, is evident in all regions. In January of 1978, the Canadian unemployment rate for young men was 15.8 per cent; for young women, 13.9 per cent. This compares with rates for men over 25 years of 5 per cent and for women over 25 years, of 7.5 per cent. The impact is most dramatic in the poorest regions, where youth unemployment frequently rises to levels in excess of 25 and 30 per cent, and sometimes higher. Quite apart from the gross waste of human resources that this represents, it creates a mood of frustration, a loss of faith in the future which reinforces the lack of confidence in the depressed region.

For much of the country, lower wages and salaries and high unemployment reinforce each other in creating and maintaining disparities. This is not true for the West. In the prairie region, except Alberta, while per capita incomes have generally been below the Canadian average, the rate of unemployment has also tended to remain two to three points below the national level; in British Columbia, which has had incomes consistently in excess of the Canadian average, unemployment has just as consistently stood well above the national level.

The reasons for these western peculiarities lie in the industrial structures of the western regions and in differences in migration patterns. The Prairies are still dependent on agriculture for employment, both directly and indirectly. Throughout the rural areas, non-farm employment is concentrated in services, transportation and trade, employment which normally shows less volatile swings. What does vary from year to year is agricultural prices and yields and this explains the erratic ups and downs in average annual incomes in the Prairies. Since the late 1960s, as well, rapid expansion has been taking place in resource based industries in the prairie region, particularly in oil in Alberta and hydro in Manitoba. These high and increasing demands for construction labour have tended to alleviate some of the unemployment, but as each project comes to an end, the threat of larger and larger unemployment arises. Construction unemployment in Manitoba in the winter of 1977-78 reached the level of one out of every three; and even in Alberta, jobs are no longer so easy to find. In the past, the harsh prairie weather has been an added inducement for migration westward into B.C. or eastward to Ontario. This has helped keep the prairie unemployment rate lower than it would be otherwise, while to some extent augmenting unemployment in B.C.

B.C. is heavily dependent on primary export industries which pay good wages but are subject to considerable fluctuations in employment. Seasonal unemployment, which is a common feature of resource industries like lumbering and fishing, also contributes to the province's high unemployment rate. By comparison, and not surprisingly, Ontario has the most stable seasonal employment patterns.

Economic welfare is measured not only by the number of jobs available and the wages paid, but also by the quality and location of the jobs. As the union president in Sudbury commented after the layoffs in the area mines announced late in 1977, the workers of Sudbury don't want to be "pack sack" miners, uprooted from their community every time demand fluctuates. The problem of ghost towns and transient workers is not new to Canada, as one can see from taking a car trip along Highway 3 through the old southern B.C. mining regions. The lack of industrial development in the hinterland resource areas means community instability. The costs of this instability fall upon the workers and contribute to the high unemployment in these regions.

A contemporary example is the case history of one Newfoundland worker who followed the advice of the present Minister of Employment and went the "packsack" route.

It is very difficult for anyone, native or newcomer, to gain any roots in Stephenville. Ten years ago after I had completed a tour of duty with the Armed Services, I returned home, only to find I was unable to find employment. Being single then, having to move to a different province did not cause any problem for me, so I moved to Toronto.

While there, I married a Stephenville girl and naturally we were interested in returning to our native home to raise our family — so when it was announced that Labrador Linerboard was being constructed, we packed up and came back.

Stephenville's future looked wonderfully bright. I got a job on the construction of the mill, and then in the mill itself. Everything was great, so we proceeded to build our new home. We invested our savings as well as mortgage money into this house. Then came the announcement "The Mill is closing".

Where am I today? Sitting here, both my wife and I unemployed, with two children, a mortgage, and no signs of employment. The whole situation is pathetic. You may ask, why not move to another province again? The answer is simple. How can I? Real estate values are down, and who would want to buy a house in an area with no industry and practically no employment? I don't want to be separated from my family, but anyway I cannot visualize any job paying enough to meet my demands here on my existing home and also pay rent in another part of Canada.

Newfoundland is my Province and Stephenville my home and I do not believe any Government has the right to point their finger at me and say, "You have to leave — you have no choice if you want to exist."

Unequal Opportunities

Income and employment disparities are not the only manifestations of the legacy of uneven Canadian development. Not only is industrial development concentrated in the industrial belt of Central Canada, but the high technology industries and those most protected by tariffs are even more concentrated in the "golden horseshoe" of southern Ontario. Two thirds of Canada's most protected industry is located in Ontario, less than a quarter in Quebec. One half of Ontario's manufacturing is "high technology" heavy industry. Even Quebec, the next most industrial province, falls way behind its neighbouring province in this measure — almost half of its manufacturing sector is in low technology, light industry. The structure of manufacturing concentration as well as the concentration itself both contribute to higher instability and slower development of the hinterland regions. We will return to this problem later in chapter 2.

The related aspect of this concentration of manufacturing and, in particular, of higher technology industry in southern Ontario is that it denies to the people in the hinterland regions equal employment opportunities in what economists call "higher order" activities — research and development, engineering and technical occupations. If people living in the Maritimes, the Prairies or B.C. want to pursue such occupations, a large percentage must migrate to Central Canada. This is one way in which regional disparities of income are maintained, since the investment in education provided in the outlying regions migrates with the individual to the centralized region.

The gross disparities in higher order activities by region can be clearly shown by two measures, the concentration of research and development (R & D) and the concentration of head offices. In 1973, over half of all R & D expenditures were made in Ontario and a quarter were made in Quebec; in the Prairies there were expenditures of less than 15 per cent, in B.C., less than 10 per cent and in the Atlantic region, less than 5 per cent. The same pattern is shown in R & D contacts of private companies with the National Research Council in 1975:

Table 1-3

R & D CONTACTS OF PRIVATE COMPANIES WITH THE NRC, 1975*

Region	Number	%
Atlantic	2	2
Quebec	32	33
Ontario**	50	52
Prairies	5	5
B.C.	8	8

 * Excludes contacts by head offices of large Canada-wide corporations.
 ** Excludes contacts by companies located in Ottawa.

A similar concentration of opportunities is reflected in the distribution of head offices, as indicated in the following table:

Table 1-4

REGIONAL DISTRIBUTION OF HEAD OFFICES OF PUBLIC COMPANIES, 1975.

Region	Head Offices Manufacturing and Construction	Sales and Service
	%	%
Atlantic	5.3	4.7
Quebec	28.9	18.9
Ontario*	47.1	45.8
Prairies	7.1	13.1
B.C.	11.5	17.5

 * Includes the Ottawa-Hull Urban System

The result of this concentration of opportunities has been a persistent "brain drain" and education drain to Central Canada, particularly from the Atlantic and western regions.

The question of opportunities presents a special challenge to Quebec because of linguistic and cultural differences. It has meant that many Francophones who wished to pursue careers in scientific, technical and management fields have had to sacrifice their cultural and linguistic heritage, particularly since even in Montreal-based companies, English has been the language of higher order activities. It should not be found surprising, therefore, that the recent wave of technically trained Québécois graduates have turned to the provincial government for aggressive expansion of the role of the public sector and have embraced the cause of separatism.

Migration and Social Indicators

Higher unemployment, lower and more unstable income and fewer opportunities are the characteristics of regional disparities in Canada. Forced migration — "going down the road" as Maritimers call it — is the result. This is not to suggest that anybody should be prevented from migrating in search of his or her destiny, but the outward migration of people from certain regions has been pronounced and continuous. The Atlantic region has been the worst affected. Between 1961 and 1971 almost one half of the natural increase in the Maritimes has migrated out of the region. The Prairies have also been severely affected. Saskatchewan has been the hardest hit; the province lost all of its natural increase in the 1961 to 1971 period because the decline in agricultural employment was only just offset by the increase in other employment opportunities. Only Alberta was able to maintain its natural increase. Most of the outmigration from both regions has been to Ontario and B.C. However, more recently, the economic stagnation that has set in in B.C. has stopped the flow to that province.

There are other manifestations of regionalism in Canada. In the Atlantic provinces, the lower incomes are aggravated by a higher cost of living except in housing. If one uses as measures of social welfare, the number of telephones, infant mortality, poverty, number of doctors per 100,000 inhabitants, education expenditure or almost any of the other indicators, the picture is again one of persistent disparities, with the Atlantic region trailing on almost all counts and Ontario just as consistently leading.

Political and Economic Consequences of Regional Disparities

Even if one doesn't consider the breakup of Canada as either a likely or particularly disastrous consequence of regional disparities, the economic costs to the have provinces that arise from those disparities are signficant and growing. They take two forms, the burden of redistribution and the costs of overconcentration. Redistribution manifests itself in unemployment insurance payments, Department of Regional Economic Expansion (DREE) expenditures, tax equalization payments and Canada Assistance Payments. These must be paid from the taxes of the richer regions, yet without these transfers, consumers in the depressed regions are unable to buy the manufactures of Central Canada.

There are additional direct costs to growth and concentration of population and economic activity in already developed and urbanized regions. One of these is the cost of providing social services, roads, sewage and water, health care and recreation facilities to large urban centres. Studies in both Europe and the United States indicate that the most efficient urban population size (that is, the size that costs the taxpayer the least) is in the neighbourhood of 100,000 to 150,000. Even allowing for a wide margin of error in these estimates, urban agglomerations of more than 350,000 are bound to run into increasing costs and decreasing amenities.

At the same time, the massive migration that results from the depopulation of the depressed regions and the rural areas is a contributing factor to other social and economic problems. In those provinces in Canada with high rates of inmigration, divorce and suicide rates are high and rising. Urban sprawl, centre core poverty ghettos and traffic congestion are symptomatic of the uneven development that has characterized Canada's economic growth. There is no simple solution to these problems but without the development of an effective regional policy in Canada, there is no solution at all.

Summary

In its obsession with national unity, the federal government has persistently ignored one of the major contributing causes to political fragmentation, the wide disparities in income and opportunity that have been a constant source of grievance for the hinterland regions of Canada. These disparities, as has been shown, are not only very real, but they are very large. In spite of redistribution through income transfers, income taxes and large scale labour force migration, they remain large. While the most visible impact has been on the residents of the depressed regions, the costs of making Confederation tolerable to these regions has had to be borne by the richer regions, both in financing the transfers and in absorbing the financial and social costs of increased concentration in their urban centres.

Any lasting solution to the national unity question must, therefore, include a national assault on disparities of income and unemployment which arise out of the basic and historic structure of the Canadian economy. To comprehend the magnitude of the problem one must first understand its nature and dimensions — in short, the basic structure of Canada's regions.

2
The Regions:
The Structure of Inequality

The problem of regional disparities is engrained in the structure of the Canadian economy. At the base of the structure are the regions themselves, each with its own structural economic problems which, taken together, add up to inequality of income and opportunity. But each region is unique, and each faces different challenges. A good grasp of the economic structure of each of the regions is necessary to comprehend the nature and magnitude of these problems and challenges.

The Atlantic Region

> We have the resources. God was good to us when He made Newfoundland. Our coastal waters are literally alive with fish of all kinds.... We have the greatest seal-herds in the world...., Our water power, both in Newfoundland and Labrador, have already developed vast hydro-electric power for industrial and commercial purposes, and are capable of many times their present yield. We have great timber reserves.... Our whole island is known to be valuably mineralized....
>
> We have the resources to make us one of the greatest small nations of the earth.... Capitalists will discover our vast heritage of natural wealth, and their capital will pour in upon Newfoundland and Labrador to exploit these resources, make great profits for themselves, and bring enduring prosperity to Newfoundlanders.

Smallwood's judgment in this excerpt owes more to his uncritical exuberance than it does to objective reality but then the framers of Confederation from the Maritimes and Quebec were equally enthusiastic when promoting the prospects of their regions in the new nation. Nevertheless, the reality of Newfoundland and the Atlantic provinces today is another question.

The Atlantic provinces, including Newfoundland, have a common heritage in their association with the Atlantic trade and natural resource exploitation for export, beginning with the cod fisheries, timber and shipbuilding, mining and more recently, pulp and paper. But the undeniable fact is that over the last half century or so, neither the resource industries nor manufacturing have expanded sufficiently to offset the contraction in agriculture. The main source of new employment growth in this period has been in the service industries, including government. As two observers have noted, what unites these provinces is that they face common "problems of transportation disadvantages vis-à-vis central Canada ... a declining growth rate and [they] look largely to new mineral development for future growth". In short, Atlantic Canada is still a resource dependent region, despite the fact that it is wanting in easily exploitable new resources.

The low rate of growth in the twentieth century has left the region well behind the rest of the country. As Table 2-1 shows, personal income per capita, earned income per capita, value added in manufacturing per capita, investment per capita and labour force participation have consistently remained well below the Canadian average, while unemployment rates have stood markedly higher.

Disparities with the national level are even more formidable in the depressed subregions of the Atlantic provinces. Beyond the St. John's-Avalon Peninsular area of Newfoundland, incomes are only two-thirds those on the peninsula, and unemployment is 20 per cent higher.

Table 2-1

REGIONAL DISPARITY INDICATORS: ATLANTIC REGION
Canada = 100

	1960-69	1970-71	1972-76
Personal Income per capita	68.7	71.9	74.1
Earned Income per capita	65.7	68.9	67.5
	1960-69	*1970-72*	*1973-76*
Labour Force Participation Rate	87.5	85.6	87.7
Unemployment Rate	167.1	135.4	160.3
Investment per capita	77.2	89.1	81.5
	1960-69	*1970*	*1971-75*
Value Added in Manufacturing, per capita	35.1	37.7	39.5

Northern New Brunswick forms a similar depressed sub-region as regards income and unemployment when compared with Southern New Brunswick. In Cape Breton, Nova Scotia, incomes are about 15 per cent below the level in the Halifax area, and unemployment rates are almost double.

Table 2-2

SUBREGIONAL DISPARITIES: NOVA SCOTIA

	Halifax	Cape Breton
Unemployment rate (1976)	7.2	12.7
Participation rate (1976)	64.4	49.0
Average Income as a % of Canada (1974)	99.0	85.2

One way of looking at the problem in the Maritimes is to compare the industrial structure of the Atlantic region with that of the Canadian average. The following table compares the structure of labour force distribution in the Atlantic region to that of Canada as a whole.

Table 2-3

PERCENTAGE LABOUR FORCE DISTRIBUTION BY INDUSTRY: 1971

	Atlantic Region %	*Canada* %
Agriculture	3.0	5.6
Other Primary[a]	6.2	2.8
Manufacturing	14.2	19.8
Food and beverages	5.6	2.8
Wood and paper	3.2	2.6
Metal[b]	2.6	5.8
Electrical	.4	1.4
Petroleum, coal and chemicals	.6	1.1
Construction	7.9	6.2
Transportation and Communication	9.4	7.8
Trade	15.3	14.7
Finance and Insurance	2.6	4.2
Personal and Business Service	22.6	23.7
Public Service	11.0	7.4
Unspecified	7.9	7.9

a includes forestry, fishing, trapping, mining, quarrying and oil wells

b includes primary metal, metal fabrication, machinery and transportation equipment manufacture

A number of points should be noted. The Atlantic provinces have a higher reliance, more than double the Canadian average, on primary industries other than agriculture. Of particular importance is the fisheries (itself 2.4 per cent of the labour force). The remainder are more equally divided between forestry and mining, with, of course, provincial specialization. None of these industries is particularly healthy at the moment, given the depressed world markets for pulp and paper and non-ferrous metals, and this is compounded by depleted fish stocks. Fish catches have fallen by half between 1968 and 1978 as a result of stock depletion through over-fishing, primarily by foreign countries. As a result, job opportunities within the industry have declined by an estimated 10,000. Although Canada's imposition of the 200-mile limit and restrictions of foreign catches should bring about a gradual recovery in stocks, it may be some years before the industry can recover and expand. Resurrection of fishing will require a massive investment in freezer-trawlers and new technology. However, if the expansion takes place under large multinational corporations, the existing pattern of low wage, seasonal employment and the export of profits and deep sea jobs will continue, perpetuating regional underdevelopment. Yet this is the direction the Atlantic provinces appear to be supporting, despite discouragement from Ottawa.

Agriculture, particularly potato-growing, is the most important industry in Prince Edward Island, but like agriculture throughout the country, it has been plagued by fluctuating demand and prices and the problem of the cost-price squeeze, the result of selling on competitive world markets while buying farm inputs on monopolistic and tariff-protected markets. Throughout the Atlantic region in the last few years, costs have been escalating at rates of between 10 and 20 per cent a year. The resulting uncertain and unstable incomes have, along with technological changes, reduced employment in the P.E.I. potato industry by over 75 per cent in the last 20 years. A smaller decline in agricultural employment has been occurring in the other provinces.

The Atlantic manufacturing sector is small relative to the Canadian average. The percentage of the labour force employed in this sector is only three-quarters the level in Canada generally, and less than 60 per cent of the Ontario level. The problems are even more formidable in the structure of manufacturing. Two thirds of the

Atlantic's manufacturing employment is in food and forest processing. Its share of the higher technology and growth industries in manufacturing, the metal, electrical and chemical sectors, is a mere 40 per cent of the Canadian average. Included in this is the troubled Sydney Steel Company (Sysco) which will require massive public investment to remain in the market.

The Nova Scotia government took over Sysco from the multinational Hawker Siddeley Company when that company planned to abandon the plant for alternative locations in Central Canada and the U.S. It had become unprofitable, which is hardly surprising, considering that in the six years until 1964 that the company owned the plant, almost nothing was spent on adapting and modernizing it, in spite of net profits in excess of $12 million. Profits earned in the region were funnelled off to investment elsewhere. Now the public will have to absorb the costs of rebuilding, but this is precarious because of the discriminatory rail rates inhibiting the exports of finished products, the decline in tariff protection from offshore competition, the current depression and the lack of any national economic policy.

The Atlantic region also faces the worst energy costs in the country because of its limited — except in Labrador — conventional hydro potential. Energy costs have been aggravated by the Maritimes' reliance on offshore oil for fuel and electricity (dating from the days of cheap oil), at the same time as they have allowed their coal industry to decay.

Perhaps the clearest indicator of the depressed state of this region is the size of the government sector relative to other employers: in the Atlantic provinces its relative size is one and a half times the Canadian average. It appears that one of the few industries attracted to the region is the federal government, which has attempted to shore up employment in the region without having to develop or adopt any coherent national economic policy.

Quebec

Quebec suffers from a dual disparity — economic and cultural-linguistic. On its own, neither disparity would likely fuel a strong and committed independence movement. After all, the Maritimes are economically more disadvantaged than Quebec and there are numerous other ethnic-linguistic groups in Canada with much more restricted access to economic opportunity than the French Canadian. But the combination of lower incomes and higher unemployment than the Canadian average, with lack of opportunities for Francophones in the higher order activities, has produced the aggressive, nationalist climate that provided the background for the 1976 Parti Québécois electoral victory.

Quebec's economic origins lie in the French fur trade. But with the British conquest, the merger of the North West Fur Company with the Hudson Bay Company and the westward migration of the trade, the economy began converting to timber and agriculture, at first wheat and grain, but after devastation in the early nineteenth century by rust and insects, to livestock and dairy. The growth in demand for consumer goods also provided the impetus for the growth of light consumer goods industries — boots and shoes, bakeries, tailors and clothiers, tanneries, textiles, tobacco products, butter and cheese and furniture. The continuance of this trend presents the province with a problem of industrial structure — a dependence on low growth and low technology industries subject to fierce competition from low wage, underdeveloped countries.

Although Quebec has large mineral and pulp and paper sectors, these industries are capital intensive, employing a small percentage of the labour force and are badly depressed under current economic conditions. This explains the high rates of unemployment in the northern and northwestern parts of the province; in March 1978, it ranged 16 per cent in the far north to 25 per cent in the Rouyn-Noranda region.

The statistical record of Quebec's economic performance, when compared to the national norm, shows little reason for optimism.

Table 2-4

REGIONAL DISPARITY INDICATORS: QUEBEC
Canada = 100

	1960-69	1970-71	1972-76
Personal Income per capita	89.2	89.0	91.0
Earned Income per capita	89.0	88.2	89.0
	1960-69	*1970-72*	*1973-76*
Labour Force Participation Rate	98.0	97.3	96.5
Unemployment	134.0	131.2	125.4
Investment per capita	80.8	74.4	82.6
	1960-69	*1970*	*1971-75*
Value Added in Manufacturing, per capita	101.1	102.4	97.7

What is more worrisome is the structure of the manufacturing sector, with its heavy concentration in light consumer non-durables. In 1971, 40 per cent of employment in manufacturing was in food and beverages, clothing, textiles, leather and furniture. The 1977 *Financial Post Report* notes that 65 per cent of all manufacturing shipments are of traditional non-durable products. While manufacturing employs a higher percentage of the labour force than the Canadian average, the percentage in heavy industry and the growth sectors of manufacturing is below the average, about half the Ontario level. This means that Quebec is twice as dependent on slow growth manufacturing as its western neighbour. Some of these comparisons are evident in the following table:

Table 2-5

PERCENTAGE LABOUR FORCE DISTRIBUTION BY INDUSTRY: 1971

	Quebec %		Canada %
Agriculture	3.4		5.6
Other Primary	2.3		2.8
Manufacturing	23.1		19.8
Food and beverages		2.8	2.8
Light, non-durables[a]		6.3	2.9
Wood and Paper		2.9	2.6
Metal manufactures		4.7	5.8
Electrical		1.5	1.4
Petroleum, coal and chemicals		1.3	1.1
Construction	5.5		6.2
Transportation and Communication	7.9		7.8
Trade	13.6		14.7
Finance and Insurance	4.2		4.2
Personal and Business Service	24.0		23.7
Public Service	6.5		7.4
Unspecified	9.5		7.9

a includes textiles, knitting mills, clothing, leather and furniture. For other definitions, see Table 2-3

The result of Quebec's manufacturing structure is slow growth in employment and ultimately in population. Quebec's growth rate, for instance, has been about half of Ontario's in recent years. But more importantly, it means a constrained growth in opportunities for the young and — since the expansion of education facilities in the early 1960s — for well-trained Francophones who are not willing to give up their language and culture to seek advancement in Quebec or, more commonly, elsewhere. However, with the westward movement of economic activity, the portents are not auspicious. A quarter century ago, Montreal outstripped Toronto in head offices by 20 per cent. Now the position is drastically reversed; Toronto outnumbers Montreal two to one, and the flow continues. Despite the controversial decision by Sun Life to move its head office to Toronto from Montreal (ostensibly because of the French language legislation), the company was only doing what numerous others have been doing, in a more dignified and quiet fashion, for years.

Many separatists view this westward movement of head offices with mixed feelings. Head offices provide business for a host of other business services — advertising, printing, accounting, finance, data processing and merchandising. They also provide jobs. But this is where the Montreal structure is vulnerable. Higher management was and is dominated by Anglophones.

> As regards French relative to English participation in management, even the Montréal Chambre de Commerce complained about "the Anglophone domination of economic decision-making centres ... which has the result of directly favouring investment in Anglophone areas as well as the development of companies and services owned by members of the same Anglophone linguistic group." ... In 1971 only 15 % of head office employees earning more than $22,000 a year were of French mother tongue. In addition, the individuals of French mother tongue who reach the managerial level usually play secondary roles.

The Sun Life experience is a case in point. Less than 10 per cent of the Board of Directors are Francophones. Indeed, the Anglophone domination of the firm stretches down through a high proportion of the company's labour force, leaving only a small proportion, around 20 per cent of the lowest level jobs, open to French-speaking Quebecers. Sun Life may have been an extreme example of Anglophone dominance in Quebec but the pattern is not atypical. Head office personnel of the Royal Bank and of the Bank of Montreal are equally lacking in francophone representation. (It might be expected that the passage of Bill 101 will change that situation, but there are reasons to doubt this.) As noted in the last chapter, the lack of higher level opportunity is compounded by the low proportion of research and development in the province.

It is this isolation from economic power as much as any other factor that has led the rising middle class of educated and trained Québécois to endorse an activist public presence in industry — through agencies such as the Societé Générale de Financement du Québec (a general financing agency) and government corporations in mining, forestry, steel, petroleum and the James Bay project in hydro electricity. While none of these are P.Q. initiatives, they represent the institutional attempts of the French Canadians to break out of their dependency relationship upon Anglophone decision-making.

The Quebec government must not worry merely about the trends of the past. It must also concern itself with the threat to the Quebec economy of current trends in Canadian trade and tariff policy. The direction of policy in international tariff negotiations is toward supporting resource-related manufacturing (and possibly world scale technology industries, although how this is to be done is by no means clear). The hardest hit in these negotiations will inevitably be the "weak sisters" of Canadian manufacturing, the light, labour-intensive industries that are disproportionately concentrated in Quebec, and which employ well over 100,000 workers. Sacrificing such employment cannot but place an intolerable burden on the already strained economy of Quebec — in particular, those subregions of Quebec specializing in these industries, which are already plagued by low income (20 per cent below the national average) and high unemployment. The prospects are not encouraging.

Ontario

From being the biggest, the best, the brightest and the fastest, Ontario has fallen, at least relatively speaking, on hard times . . . .

On the broad economic front, Ontario faces labour-management difficulties, unemployment and probable shortages in energy and perhaps even capital. Its construction sector is weak and suffering audibly. In mining, by its own admission, it is developing new mines only quickly enough to replace about 30 % of its mined-out facilities. Regional disparities between Northern Ontario and the prosperous (and perhaps self-centred) south don't seem to be closing and despite a goodly number of government initiatives, there is a feeling of being abandoned in the eastern part of the province.

Ontario's early economic evolution was similar to Quebec's although it developed somewhat later. The significant difference, however, was that, because it was established later, in closer proximity to the United States' industrial and coal mining regions, and with an agricultural sector that had larger, more prosperous and more capital intensive farm units, Ontario very early maintained a lead in heavy, high technology industry, a lead which has become accentuated over time. Like Quebec, Ontario's northern hinterland has concentrated on resource extraction of minerals and pulp and paper. In the current economic situation the same depressed conditions exist in Ontario as in Quebec.

Obviously, all is not well in favoured Ontario, and not just outside the southern industrialized belt. In the four mid-winter months of 1977-78, more than 10,000 workers were laid off in Ontario, a high proportion of them in manufacturing. In March 1978, unemployment in Windsor reached over 11 per cent and in St. Catharines-Niagara, over 13 per cent. It may be the weakening position of Ontario that explains the marginal narrowing in differentials between Ontario and the Canadian average.

In fact, Ontario is a microcosm of the regional inequalities of Canada. In the North, the same problems arise as in the northern resource exploitation communities across the country: high paying but unstable jobs (the mining industry has been described as "manic-depressive") and isolated single industry communities surrounded by pockets of native poverty (and aggravated by the destruction of native renewable resources through wasteful resource usage and pollution). In March 1978, in the region around Georgian Bay and north, including Sudbury and Sault-Ste-Marie, the average rate of unemployment was 34 per cent higher than the Ontario average and 63 per cent higher than in Toronto. Sudbury's unemployment rate was almost double that of the Ontario capital.

Northern Ontario has been described as a "crown colony", whose decision-making and institutions of financial control are centred in Toronto or in foreign multinationals. Transportation rates discriminate against economic diversification. Population is stagnant; opportunities for young people, particularly those with higher formal education, are almost non-existent. There are also complaints of a shortage of skilled labour, but with the chronic instability of the resource industries, the unions and the young people are not anxious to embark

Table 2-6

REGIONAL DISPARITY INDICATORS: ONTARIO
Canada=100

	1960-69	1970-71	1972-76
Personal Income per capita	117.1	117.3	111.5
Earned Income per capita	118.4	119.0	114.2
	1960-69	1970-72	1973-76
Labour Force Participation Rate	104.5	104.1	104.5
Unemployment Rate	73.1	76.8	82.5
Investment per capita	102.8	106.2	97.0
	1960-60	1970	1971-75
Value Added in Manufacturing, per capita	150.7	148.1	148.4

on an expansion of apprenticeship programs which may only swell the unemployed in the next downturn. At present, the region is depressed by the general depression in mining and pulp and paper production. The massive layoffs at Sudbury have helped at least to dramatize the region's uncertain future and the poor state of the pulp and paper industry is perhaps a mixed curse: given the poor record of provincial reforestation, it may help delay for a few years the approaching timber shortages.

Eastern Ontario shares many of the same structural problems as Quebec. It has the same concentration in light manufacturing, including the textile and electronic

Table 2-7

PERCENTAGE LABOUR FORCE DISTRIBUTION BY INDUSTRY: 1971

	Ontario %	Canada %
Agriculture	3.9	5.6
Forestry, fishing, trapping	.3	1.2
Mining, quarrying and oil wells	1.2	1.6
Manufacturing	24.4	19.8
Food and beverages	2.5	2.8
Light, non-durables	2.7	2.9
Wood and paper	1.9	2.6
Metal manufactures	9.1	5.8
Electrical	2.2	1.4
Petroleum, coal and chemicals	1.5	1.1
Construction	6.1	6.2
Transportation and Communications	6.6	7.8
Trade	14.8	14.7
Finance and Insurance	4.6	4.2
Personal and Business Service	23.5	23.7
Public Service	7.4	7.4
Unspecified	7.1	7.9

industries, and the same agricultural weaknesses resulting from expanding non-agricultural land use and the flood of cheap food imports. This is also true of the province as a whole, and in the last decade the number of commercial farms in Ontario has declined by almost 20 per cent.

It is the industrial heartland of southern Ontario, the tariff-protected northern extension of the American industrial belt, that has provided the jobs and the incomes that make Ontario the leading province economically and that masks the subregional disparities discussed above.

Ontario has been particularly favoured by its structure of manufacturing, with the disproportionate share of heavy manufacturing, 50 per cent more important to Ontario than to Canada as a whole. But despite Ontario's advantages, there are strong indications that it may be facing the same kind of deindustrialization that stripped the Maritimes of their manufacturing vitality almost a century ago. Well over half of its manufacturing, including the heavy industry sectors and most of its large firms, is foreign controlled by companies which have little interest in developing new products or new techniques in their Ontario branch plants. Already, according to the executive director of the Science Council of Canada, the failure to develop a coherent national economic strategy is costing the country 10,000 jobs a month. And with the existing industrial structure, a large proportion of these jobs would have been in Ontario.

The Prairies

Thirty Canadian farmers leave the land every day....
Over 150,000 farmers have been pushed off the land in Western Canada in the interests of efficiency....

The majority of prairie farmers are poor, even rich farmers are poor by urban standards. In 1971, which was considered a good year, the average Saskatchewan farmer made $4,616 — half what an urban construction worker makes every year. In 1970, the year of the most recent agricultural depression, the average farm income across the prairies was $2,500 — less than a farm family would make on welfare....

The tide is ebbing now, sucking people off the land, eroding the prairie towns and villages until they collapse like sand castles. Between 1966 and 1971, Saskatchewan lost 30,000 people, and its rural population decreased by more than 50,000. Alberta is losing 5,000 rural people a year, Manitoba 3,000. Most of them move to cities; the young go east, the old go west. Almost all of them are farmers.

The Prairies are, at one and the same time, a region of both great expectations and dashed hopes, of frontier economic exuberance and the despair of economic decline. Agriculture, and particularly wheat, was the economic base upon which the prairie region was settled in the early years of the twentieth century. This base has diversified somewhat in the intervening years with the expansion of the livestock and meatpacking industry, particularly in Alberta; the development of metal and uranium mining in the northern reaches where the Canadian Shield crosses the prairie provinces; and the expansion of manufacturing and service industries to support regional consumer and agricultural needs. Now, oil and energy have become the investment frontier of the region, but agriculture remains the number one industry.

The problem is, agriculture is troubled by instability and low income. In 1977 the farmers' share of the total Canadian income dropped to its lowest point in history — 1.7 per cent. Yet in 1971, farmers made up 5.6 per cent of the Canadian labour force. Although the two figures are not directly comparable, the magnitude of the difference between them is one indication of the depressed economic picture in agriculture.

At the same time, the massive expansion in energy projects, the huge tax revenues in petroleum and natural gas, have created an economic boom of considerable dimensions in the western Prairies. As the *Financial Post* has noted, "Energy-related spending is at the heart of much of the West's economic buoyancy." But the buoyancy is precarious, much of it depending on how projects develop. The crunch will come when the sector stops expanding, which has already happened in Manitoba.

The energy related investment boom is readily apparent. Between 1973 and 1976 per capita investment was almost 30 per cent higher in the Prairies than in Canada generally, even though average incomes in the Prairies have remained at, or just below, the national average. The boom is, however, narrowly based. Manufacturing in the prairie region provides less than half the per capita income it provides in the country as a whole and less than a third it provides in Ontario. The small improvement that took place from 1972-76 was largely based on the processing of natural resources, particularly the expansion of the petrochemical industry in Alberta.

Table 2-8

REGIONAL DISPARITY INDICATORS: THE PRAIRIES
Canada=100

	1960-69	1970-71	1972-76
Personal Income per capita	94.4	92.1	98.4
Earned Income per capita	94.4	91.7	99.6
	1960-69	1970-72	1973-76
Labour Force Participation Rate	101.9	101.9	102.5
Unemployment	62.7	72.1	58.7
Investment per capita	123.8	113.5	129.0
	1960-69	1970	1971-75
Manufacturing Value Added per capita	39.9	41.7	44.7

Table 2-9

PERCENTAGE LABOUR FORCE DISTRIBUTION BY INDUSTRY: 1971

	Prairies %	*Canada* %
Agriculture	15.9	5.6
Forestry, fishing and trapping	.4	1.2
Mining, quarrying and oil wells	2.8	1.6
Manufacturing	9.5	19.8
Food and beverages	2.4	2.8
Light, non-durables	1.1	2.9
Wood and paper	.8	2.6
Metal manufactures	2.6	5.8
Electrical	.3	1.4
Petroleum, coal and chemicals	.7	1.1
Construction	6.3	6.2
Transportation and Communications	8.3	7.8
Trade	15.0	14.7
Finance and Insurance	3.5	4.2
Personal and Business Service	23.4	23.7
Public Service	7.8	7.4
Unspecified	7.2	7.9

Excepting the diverse service sector, agriculture remains the leading employer in the prairie region. It is in an unhealthy state. The traditional complaint of the western farmer has been his competitive inferiority — selling on a competitive world market and buying on a protected domestic market. In fact, the problem is much more complex. Canada has followed a "cheap food" policy and has consistently concentrated "aid" to the farmer in programs that would improve productivity or shift production from products in surplus internationally to those where demand was growing. Quite apart from the glaring errors made by government prognosticators (such as encouraging a 40 per cent increase in beef herds between 1969 and 1974 in time to feed a world surplus, and a cut-back in cereal production just before world shortages pushed grain prices to record highs), the purpose of these policies has been to maintain low food prices with minimum government support. Some support has been provided in the 1970s by Eugene Whelan's supply management and marketing board policies, which have gone some way toward stabilizing incomes at remunerative levels for some products, including eggs, milk and poultry. But for the main western products, grain and cattle, markets remain unfettered — with all the resulting instabilities of price and sales and with them, farm incomes. The cattle industry is at its lowest ebb since the 1930s and grain prices have fallen in spite of the devaluation of the Canadian dollar.

On the other side of the market, the farmer faces the price-fixing oligopoly of "agribusiness" — described by Don Mitchell in *The Politics of Food* as "all industries and agencies which own, manage or profit from activities directly related to agriculture" — and protected oligopolistic manufacturers and major sales outlets like the supermarket chains. Squeezed between production and living costs and low and unstable prices and incomes, farmers have been leaving the land in a massive outmigration. This has also meant a precariously unstable existence for prairie-based farm machinery and agricultural service industries. The *Financial Post* reports that "The industry's strength is that it makes equipment designed especially for local conditions. But the weakness is that it depends on how much money local farmers have to spend."

As long as energy investment continues, the Prairies' economic position will appear bright, despite the agricultural problems. Manitoba is already heading into decline as hydro investment slows, depressed markets cripple the nickel and pulp and paper industries, and reckless contractionist policies are carried out by the right-wing Conservative provincial government elected in 1977. The future of the region will depend largely on the success of the development strategies now being pursued by the Alberta and Saskatchewan governments, which is discussed in chapter 4.

British Columbia

Connections between the lower mainland (which should somehow be thought of as including our capital city Victoria) and the rest of the province have always been grotesque. From a mining or pulp town, for instance, the lines of communications go first to New York or London or Tokyo and then to Greater Vancouver. For lumber towns it is best to go through Chicago or even Cedar Rapids, Iowa . . . . Coal? For action call Kaiser in San Francisco. To ask what happened to the Columbia River, don't phone Victoria, get hold of Washington, D.C., although they may not answer because they're still laughing too hard.

When the framers of the national policy a century ago decried Canada's natural future as a "hewer of wood and drawer of water", British Columbia was just a new member of a young confederation, suffering from a declining gold industry and desperately seeking a new economic role. British Columbia is now the hewer of wood and a drawer of minerals, *par excellence*. Natural resources have made B.C. one of the "have" provinces. They have been her strength — and her weakness. They have provided high incomes, but have also led to high unemployment.

The forest industry is highly cyclical. It is also very capital intensive, particularly in the pulp and paper sector. The same is true of the mining industry, the other primary mainstay of the B.C. economy. But, like all capital intensive, primary resource extraction, direct employment is limited. Swings in these primary industries, nevertheless, have major effects on the overall level of provincial economic activity through the construction industry, which depends on the growth of new resource

Table 2-10

REGIONAL DISPARITY INDICATORS: BRITISH COLUMBIA
Canada=100

	1960-69	1970-71	1972-76
Personal Income per capita	111.9	108.7	109.0
Earned Income per capita	110.1	107.7	108.9
	1960-69	1970-72	1973-76
Labour Force Participation Rate	89.7	102.2	101.0
Unemployment	116.7	119.6	117.5
Investment per capita	129.5	136.6	116.3
	1960-69	1970	1971-75
Manufacturing Value Added per capita	88.8	79.0	84.9

developments for a significant amount of construction employment. The reliance of the province on these basic industries shows up in the distribution of the labour force.

Employment in the primary forestry industry and in wood and paper products manufacturing is close to three times the national levels. B.C. lags in all other manufacturing sectors, however. The province's dependence on the provincial forests is comparable to the Prairies' dependence on agriculture. Paradoxically, it is the postwar success in wood-related industries that poses threats to B.C.'s status as a have province. The rapid and profitable expansion of the industry, compounded by excessively low taxes on natural resource rents, permitted a sharing of inflated profits with labour in the form of high wages. This expansion contributes to the high per capita incomes and wages, yet acts as a formidable barrier to the expansion of other manufacturing industries while providing strong incentives to the growth of service industries.

Table 2-11

PERCENTAGE LABOUR FORCE DISTRIBUTION BY INDUSTRY: 1971

	British Columbia %	Canada %
Agriculture	2.5	5.6
Forestry, fishing and trapping	3.4	1.2
Mining, quarrying and oil wells	1.6	1.6
Manufacturing	16.1	19.8
Food and beverages	2.2	2.8
Light, non-durables	.7	2.9
Wood and paper	6.9	2.6
Metal manufactures	3.3	5.8
Electrical	.4	1.4
Petroleum, coal and chemicals	.5	1.1
Construction	7.0	6.2
Transportation and Communications	9.5	7.8
Trade	16.2	14.7
Finance and Insurance	4.6	4.2
Personal and Business Service	24.8	23.7
Public Service	6.3	7.4
Unspecified	7.4	7.9

The problems arise when the forest industry falls back because of the depletion of new and readily available supplies of trees, a decline in external demand or the rise in imports of competitive supplies from other countries. All of these factors, plus the growing obsolescence of much B.C. plant and equipment, are presently depressing the industry. Badly needed new investment to upgrade plants may return the industry to competitiveness, but it is also likely that it will be labour saving — that is, jobs will not grow proportionately, which will compound the trade-off between employment and income. In the short run, the construction industry may also be reprieved for another round of the boom-bust cycle, but how long this can last is uncertain.

While the province as a whole is dependent on the cyclical patterns of resource exploitation it is the central interior regions of the province, those most specialized in resource extraction, where the effects are most pronounced. In early 1978, unemployment in the interior was a third higher than in the province as a whole and over 40 per cent higher than in Vancouver.

The North: History as the Present

Look at the housing where transient government staff live. And look at the housing where the Indian people live.... Look at where the Bay store is, right on top of the highest point of land. Do you think that this is the way the Indian people chose to have this community?
...

Do you think people chose to live in rental houses owned by the government, instead of in houses they built for themselves? Do you think they chose to have a system of justice which often they cannot understand and which does not allow them to help their own people and deal with their own problems? A system which punishes the Indians for stealing from the Bay, but does not punish the Bay for stealing from the Indians? Do you think that they chose to become cheap labour for oil companies, construction companies, and government instead of working for themselves and developing their own economy in their own way? ...

For a while it seemed that we might escape the greed of the southern system .... If our Indian nation is being destroyed so that poor people of the world might get a chance to share the world's riches, then as Indian people, I am sure that we would seriously consider giving up our resources. But do you really expect us to give up our life and our lands so that those few people who are the richest and the most powerful in the world today can maintain and defend their own immoral position of privilege?

The Northern reaches of Canada have become the example, without peer, of inequality and disparity between the client economy of the numerous native peoples and the affluent extension of the southern economy in the natural resource extraction industries and among government administrators. This pattern of inequality is not restricted to the Northwest Territories and Yukon but covers the northern areas of each province as well. Reliable statistics on the whole northern region are not available to document this phenomenon of underdevelopment but health statistics provide some indication. In 1964, the child mortality rate of Indian children was 13 times the average Canadian rate. The average age of death of N.W.T. Inuit was 19.3 years, for Indians, 29.9, compared to the Canadian average of 61 years. Female mortality rates of Indians were 5 times the Canadian average, and so on. Per capita incomes for natives in the N.W.T. in 1969 were estimated at around $1,100, a little over a third of the level (estimated at $3,000), for other residents of the N.W.T., which was slightly higher than the Canadian average. Production per capita was much higher, $5,311 in 1970, and the difference between this figure and the per capita income is a measure of the drain to the South of the value of production in the North. Northern Manitoba data may also be taken as indicative. Native participation in the Northern Manitoba labour force is minimal: the participation rate, i.e. the proportion of working-age people in the labour force, is only in the range of 29 per cent, a fraction of the southern rate. It is estimated that only 43 per cent of all Indians over 15 years of age have ever worked in the labour market; since the native population makes up a significantly higher proportion of the population in the North than elsewhere these figures give some idea of the magnitude of the inequity problem. The fact is that the native population has never had in recent years the economic opportunity to make a meaningful contribution to the economy.

This was not always true. Canada was built on the economic contribution of the native population. The boundaries of Canada were created by the fur trade, for which the native peoples provided the largest part of the productive labour force. If we take the western Arctic as typical, the fur trader (supplemented by missionaries and police representing church and state), continued until a generation ago to be the point of contact between the indigenous Dene and Inuit peoples and the Canadian South. By the early 1950s, the collapse of the fur trade and rising interest in the strategic and resource values of the North led to federal intervention in the region. The traditional economy was destroyed, to be replaced by the welfare system, which shored up a mixed wage/hunting and trapping economy. Thus what has happened as late as 20 or so years ago in the North is just a repetition of the destruction of the traditional native economies in the South that resulted from their integration with the metropolitan fur trade.

The traditional native economy based on hunting and trapping provided a natural complement to the interests of the commercial fur interests. The natives became increasingly dependent on the fur trade for tools, some provisions and supplies and consumer goods. When the trade collapsed in the South, as it did at various times in the nineteenth century, depending on the location, the native population was thrown into destitution. The form of "welfare state" at this time was the reserve, an institution to maintain the native people at subsistence levels at minimum cost to the state. The more northerly one goes, the later the fur trade lasted as the dominant economic mode.

In the wake of the fur trade came new forms of resource exploitation — mining, logging and pulp and paper, and more recently hydro, oil and gas development. This new type of resource exploitation has created a dualistic structure in the North, with the native population living at or near subsistence levels alongside but separated from enclaves of relatively well-off whites, commonly southerners. When the development phase of these resource exploitation projects is completed, the imported construction workers pack up and head south again. When the mine is exhausted, the non-local miners pack up and head for some new mine, some new community. The original inhabitants of the North do not have such options.

In the western Arctic, the drama is one not of history but of our own day. Ever since oil was discovered on the north slope of Alaska in the 1960s, the multinational oil corporations have turned their attention to the potential of the Canadian Arctic, with the encouragement of the Canadian government. This presents a new challenge to the welfare of the indigenous northerners. Oil exploration is not restricted to the sparse settlements, as the government administration and mine communities were, but competes for the land with the native hunter and trapper. The industry is also completely divorced from the northern economy, and does not even provide significant unskilled wage labour opportunities for northern inhabitants.

It is often suggested that, regardless of the problems, resource development must take place and the northern population integrated into the white wage market if the North is not to degenerate further into a client, welfare dependency. There are two major problems with this position. The first is that the dependence is first and foremost the result of past incursions of southern "development". And second, what happens when the exhaustible resources run out, as they inevitably must?

The negative impact of "development" on northern welfare is well illustrated by Dr. Peter Usher's intensive study of the Banksland Inuit trapping economy in the mid-1960s. The Bankslanders had a per capita income close to the Canadian average and a viable, prosperous trapping economy. The oil companies came, offering jobs worth approximately half as much as the Inuit were already making in trapping. Moreover, the Bankslanders were concerned that the exploration crews and seismic operations posed a major threat to the environment that supported their economy. Clearly, the oil and gas industry is no substitute for the development of traditional industries. In fact, as evidence before the Berger inquiry by Father Lou Menez pointed out, "southern development" resulted in the de-development of the local native economy of Fort Resolution, and had a detrimental impact on fur, river transport, sawmilling and fishing.

Robert Davis and Mark Zannis in their analysis of Canadian northern strategy, *The Genocide Machine in Canada*, sum up the future concisely:

> When the oil and gas cartel has pulled out, Canada will be faced with the economic burden of supporting a greatly-expanded native population in the Arctic which would have no economic base and no possibilities of building one. Nor would a return to a subsistence hunting economy be possible. The welfare bill would be tremendous, the alienation, bitterness and hostility of the people of the North complete.

The distortion of the resource-based enclave economy is readily apparent in the statistics on economic activity in the two northern territories. The influence of the natural resource exploitation is dramatic, as shown by the high per capita investment and the relative concentration of employment in the mining sector, over seven times the average Canadian level. But the other side of the inequality is evident in the minimal size of the manufacturing sector, the relatively high proportion of the labour force engaged in fishing and trapping (comparable to the Atlantic region) and the extremely high percentage of the labour force in government employment (18.4 per cent of the labour force, two and a half times the average Canadian level).

The current phase of southern economic expansion into the northern hinterland and the inequalities thereby imposed are nothing new to Canadian history — they repeat the pattern of Canadian history.

Summary

Each region in Canada has its own particular structure, its own particular problems. But there are also some common dimensions. One that has been stressed has been the instability of the resource hinterland, its dependence on external demand and its low employment potential even under more auspicious economic circumstances than at the present.

The structure of manufacturing is also extremely important because it is a key to an industrialized, self-reliant and healthy economy. The small percentage differences in employment distribution between regions may seem reassuring but provide a false impression, as the following table shows. If we take the Canadian average as the standard (and it is a very weak standard to take in comparison with other western industrialized countries), disparities in employment structure are very marked.

Ontario is not only proportionately much stronger in manufacturing but its relative strength is greatest in the growth areas and lowest in dependence on resource extraction employment. On the other hand, Quebec is relatively strongest in light, low technology manufacturing. The dependence of the Maritimes and the North on government employment and natural resource extraction is very marked, while B.C. has a strong dependence on natural resources extraction and wood and paper production. The Prairies have a weak manufacturing base but the region comes closest to the Canadian average in food and beverage manufacture although it is surprising that employment is not stronger in this sector.

These wide disparities in regional industrial structures are not accidental, but have been created and perpetuated by a century of government policy.

Table 2-12

REGIONAL EMPLOYMENT STRUCTURES

*Indexes of the Proportional Distribution
of the Regional Labour Forces
(Canada = 100)*

Industry or Sector	Atlantic	Que.	Ont.	Prairies	B.C.	Yukon and N.W.T.
Natural Resource Extraction (Excl. Agric.)	221.4	82.1	57.6	114.3	178.6	542.9
Manufacturing (total)	71.7	116.7	123.2	48.0	81.3	13.1
Food and Beverages	200.0	100.0	89.3	85.7	78.6	14.3
Light, non-durables	24.1	217.2	93.1	37.9	24.1	13.8
Wood and paper	123.1	111.5	73.1	30.8	265.4	19.2
"Growth Sector" (total)	43.4	90.4	154.2	43.4	50.6	*
Metal Manufactures	44.8	81.0	156.9	44.8	56.9	*
Electrical	28.6	107.1	157.1	21.4	28.6	*
Petroleum, coal and chemicals	54.5	118.2	136.4	63.3	45.5	*
Public Service	148.6	87.8	100.0	105.4	85.1	248.6

3
The Regional Implications of Confederation

Regionalism is not new to Canada. In fact, it is one of the reasons for Canada. Our constitution, the British North America (BNA) Act, was designed to knit together the existing British regions of North America into an integrated political and economic unit. Politically, it has been a success if only to the extent that Canada still exists as a unit. Economically, however, success has eluded us. To consider the Canadian economy as an independent, integrated, policy-making unit is a fallacy. Rather than comprising a national economy, Canada is broken up into a series of economic regions of the North American economy. This is one of the main reasons why government policy has done little to decrease disparities or more generally to stabilize and promote development of the Canadian economy.

But before we can show why our present structure and policy have been so ineffective in dealing with the problem of regionalism, a brief look at how Canada got into this position is necessary. We cannot ignore the historical evolution of our regions because disparities are deeply rooted in our past. Unless we understand the causes it is hard to see how we can develop remedial policies. And basic to any initiative is the realization that regional inequality breeds further inequality.

Before Confederation

When Europeans first came to the northern half of our continent, they found a land populated by a wide diversity of native peoples, each with its own economy and culture. As the Europeans drove west across the continent in search of furs, more and more of the native peoples were integrated into the trade and made dependent on the world market in furs. When the fur trade spread to the west coast by the early nineteenth century, the boundaries of Canada had been defined. While most of the wealth created by the trade in Canada flowed to the merchants of Montreal or to the British owners of the Hudson's Bay Company, there was a sense in which the country had a unified economy. Even so, the Atlantic region had already developed in other directions, and its economy was centred on fishing and Atlantic trade.

In the century before Confederation regional identities became increasingly differentiated. Agriculture had spread west to Ontario, which became the bread basket of Canada and a major exporter to Europe. In the Maritimes and the more northern treed areas of Quebec and Ontario, forestry had become the dominant industry. Quebec was already a divided economy. The rural agricultural areas had been devastated by rust and insect invasions which destroyed the grain industry, leaving the inhabitants a marginal existence based on small mixed farming. Quebec's native sons were driven to lumber camps both in Canada and the United States and to the textile mills of New England.

Montreal and the St. Lawrence ports were a different story. Here resided the great Tory merchant class who exported the wheat, timber and potash staples and imported the goods for consumers and producers. Mainly at public expense they built the canals that would let their ships pass to the Great Lakes, more in hopes of capturing the trade of the American frontier than of tapping Canadian output. Canadian merchants had the advantage over their American competitors in supplying

the British grain market because of British preferences
on grain and flour coming from, or at least through, the
Canadian colonies. These preferences, the "Corn
Laws", were in the form of lower tariffs on Canadian
shipments to Britain. British preferences also favoured
the timber industry, which did much to encourage the
rapid exploitation of eastern and central Canadian
forests.

Then, in the face of the Irish potato famine in the
1840s, Britain repealed its protective system, leaving the
Canadian colonies without any advantage in the British
market. The Tory merchants of Montreal were incensed
and resorted to rioting and burning down the legislative
buildings — to no avail. The loss of the protected British
market was a severe blow to the grand imperial design of
the Montreal merchants. Many got together to sign a
manifesto demanding annexation of Canada to the
United States. But the crisis was relatively short-lived. In
1854, the reciprocity treaty providing for free trade in
natural resources and products between the United
States and Canada was negotiated, giving impetus to a
north-south trade in agricultural and timber products in
both Central Canada and the Maritimes. Prosperity
seemed assured, particularly after the outbreak of the
American Civil War, when the northern States turned to
Canada for supplies to supplement their own war-
strained resources.

But there were problems on the horizon. The Canadian canals proved to be no competition for the new
American railways in the export of the products of the
western frontier. The Canadian merchants retaliated by
building their own railway system, again largely with the
help of the public purse, and leaving a legacy of public
debt. British and Canadian sympathies with the southern
cause in the U.S. Civil War did not add to Canadian-
American bonds after the war. The election of Abraham
Lincoln in 1860 had signalled the adoption by the U.S. of
a national system of protection which was to greatly re-

duce its openness to imported products. Canada was no exception. The end of the reciprocity treaty became a foregone conclusion.

Cast adrift by Britain and now again by the United States, the Canadian ruling elite (still centred in Montreal but increasingly also in Toronto, which had prospered with the American connection) was forced to search for an alternative. So were the commercial leaders of the Maritimes, who also faced loss of their free access to American markets and supplies, which were important to the region's participation in the Atlantic trade. The public debt had mounted in both regions to provide the railways designed to push the frontier for exploitation further from the seaboard. Debt-ridden, uncertain of their economic futures and pressured by the British Colonial office, which was anxious to get rid of its expensive and troublesome North American colonies now that they were of no use in the new British economic policy, the political-economic elite of the two regions met to consider alternatives.

Confederation

Barred from exploiting the American western frontier, the "Fathers of Confederation" foresaw the creation of their own western empire. Unfortunately, the thousand or so miles of barren waste known as the Canadian Shield stood in the way. Already mired in railway and canal debt for an unsuccessful transportation system, the central Canadian colonies, united since 1841, could not raise sufficient credit to go it alone with a Pacific railway.

What had the Maritimes to gain from any union, when its frontier faced to the east — to the Atlantic and its merchant trade? At this time the maritime colonies had the fourth largest merchant marine in the world, supported by the timber, fishing, sugar import and shipbuilding industries. The proposed Confederation would absorb the railway debt, help protect the region's fisheries, and would create a transportation link between the

maritime region and Central Canada, thus opening up
new markets to compensate for the end of free access to
the United States. Galt, Finance Minister of Central Canada, pushed this point in the Confederation debates:

> It is in the diversity of employment that security is
> found against those sad reverses to which every coun-
> try, depending mainly on one branch of industry, must
> always be liable.... We may therefore rejoice that, in
> the proposed Union of the British North American Pro-
> vinces we shall obtain some security against those
> providential reverses to which, as long as we are depen-
> dent on one branch of industry as a purely agricultural
> country, we must always remain exposed.

Maritimers were much less impressed with the prospects. But during this prosperous time, the linking of the
two regions did not appear to pose much of a threat. On
the contrary, it promised some specific benefits, particularly protection for the fishery interests and a market for
maritime manufacturers, some of whom were convinced
that the Atlantic region would become the manufacturing emporium of the new Confederation. Prince Edward
Islanders were more realistic about the competitive position of their island's agriculture and resisted joining the
new union for seven years. Only Newfoundland stood
more or less completely outside the economic forces encouraging a realignment of the east coast region towards
the continent and away from the Atlantic. The Maritimers were not to know at the time (although many sus-
pected it), that continental integration was to have not a
lasting developmental but an anti-developmental impact.
Galt's words proved true for Ontario, but not for the
Atlantic region.

The Confederation debate also made it very clear that
the eyes of the economic elite of Central Canada were on
the profits to be made from its own captive western frontier. Confederation of the Maritimes and Central Canada
was the instrument by which the central Canadian elite
could conquer the West for itself and fend off the impe-

rialist designs of the Americans to the south.

U.S. penetration was already threatening. The Red River Colony had developed strong commercial ties with St. Paul. British Columbia, after a rapid growth due to the gold rush, during which large public debts had been incurred for inland roads and port facilities, was faced with exhaustion of its staple gold resource. Many of its merchants, like those in the Red River Colony and the Montreal merchants a quarter of a century earlier, advocated annexation to the U.S. to jump behind the prohibitive American tariff.

But the British connection was not to be denied. Rupert's Land, comprising essentially the Canadian Prairies and the North, was bought from the Hudson's Bay Company and turned over to the new federal government. B.C. entered Confederation in 1871 on the promise of a national railway joining the Pacific Coast with the East. All that was left was to integrate these new and disparate regions into the Canadian economy. This was the goal of what has become known as the "national policy", a policy to weld this collection of very different regions into a viable economic and political unit. It required linking the regions together both physically, in terms of transportation links, and economically, to prevent American commercial interests from capturing the profits of the trade and resources of these western regions. This also required the settlement of these areas to prevent American population expansion from taking over the otherwise sparsely settled regions. These were the goals of the national policy, and they were accomplished by railways, tariffs and land settlement policies.

Confederation, however, was founded on regionalism, a concept which did not consider the regions to be equal. The Prairies were to provide a frontier for central Canadian investment, a market for eastern manufacturers and consumers for the commercial trades of the St. Lawrence merchants. It is clear that the original intent of the framers of the British North America Act was to give

AUGUSTANA LIBRARY
UNIVERSITY OF ALBERTA

the federal government the important economic development powers and leave to the provinces the powers that were considered of merely local interest. Of most importance were the federal powers of interprovincial railways, tariffs and customs (which in those pre-income tax days were the major source of government revenues), and joint powers with the provinces over agriculture and immigration. Furthermore, the whole prairie and northern regions, except Manitoba, did not have provincial status and were administered by Ottawa. The Métis leader, Louis Riel led the 1869 rebellion in opposition to federal designs on the West, demanding provincial status so that Manitoba might be an equal partner in Confederation. This could be considered the first regional protest movement in Canada, and one that had a measure of success. Just a tiny "postage stamp" province then, Manitoba was admitted to Confederation in 1870, but not as an equal partner. Unlike the other provinces, Manitoba's crown land resources were retained by the federal government as part of the senior government's strategy for opening the West. The land in the rest of the prairie and northwest region was also retained in federal hands, even after Saskatchewan and Alberta were given provincial status in 1905.

Control of the land resources was of little use to the national design if there was no transportation access to the West. The national policy required an all Canadian railway route and after several false starts and scandals, the Canadian Pacific Railway was chartered by the federal government in early 1881. The CPR was very much a triumph of public enterprise, its inspiration and much of its financing coming from the national government. The railway was given $25 million plus some 710 miles of government constructed track — worth about $38 million, 25 million acres of land, and numerous other tax, tariff and finance benefits. What grated most to westerners, however, was the monopoly clause in the agreement, which prohibited the chartering of competing lines south of the CPR line that might connect with American railways. The clause effectively delivered settlers to the mercy of the CPR transportation monopoly.

The Tariff Issue

Two of the elements of the national policy were thus in place. In fact, even before the CPR was built, the third element of the national policy had been enacted. John A. Macdonald's National Policy Tariffs were the central issue in the 1878 election. Macdonald was successful in his attempt to regain power from the Liberals, who had defeated him in 1872 over a kickback scandal involving the Pacific railway. Protectionism is usually politically popular during depressions, and the Conservative campaign was aided by the depressed economic conditions in the country during the previous five years of Liberal rule. The tariff legislation was passed in 1879. All the elements of the national policy were in place. All that was needed was the immigration to fill the West and the markets for agricultural products that would support this western expansion.

Canadian tariff policy has been one of the most persistent causes of regional protest throughout Canadian history. At this time customs income was the most important source of governmental finance: at Confederation, customs and excise taxes accounted for over 80 per cent of revenues. In 1858 the government of the United Canadas, burdened by railway debt, increased tha tariffs on manufactured goods, although Galt, the finance minister, admitted that the tariffs might also provide "incidental protection". Although the reciprocity treaty with the U.S. in effect at the time only covered raw products, the Americans considered the tariff increase a breach of the spirit of the treaty, if not of the letter, and used this as one excuse for its withdrawal from the treaty in 1865.

But when negotiations were underway for Confederation, there was considerable opposition in the Maritimes to the tariffs in effect in Canada. The eastern region lived by international commerce and protection threatened that commerce. In 1866, one year before Confederation, the Canadian colony lowered its tariffs, in large measure to reduce Maritime opposition. But it is also clear that the concept of a system of national protection of Canadian manufacturing was not widely supported by colonial leaders at the time Confederation was being debated. Between 1867 and 1878 this attitude was reversed. The tariff increases of 1858 had been primarily for revenue and incidentally for protection. The increases of 1879 were specifically for protection. Why the turnabout?

The reasons for this change in attitude have been hotly debated by Canadian historians. Some argue that there was a growing class of Canadian industrial capitalists whose influence had emerged stronger than the older elite of merchants. Others have argued that the only way the commercial capitalists and bankers could protect their investment in railways and their interregional trade was to protect the Canadian market from growing American competition by forcing trade on an east-west axis. Others have been even more specific, arguing that the CPR could never have been economical if the tariff had not forced western consumers to purchase eastern Canadian goods and thereby guarantee traffic to the railway across the barren wastes north of the Great Lakes. We can also not forget the depressed economic conditions of the 1870s. It is probable that all of these played some part in the conversion to protectionism. But whatever the reasons, the results have had a profound and lasting effect on the regional structure of the Canadian economy.

The Regional Impact of National Policy

The imposition of a system of protectionism had many of the effects that its advocates prophesized. Backed by other legislation on patents and assorted bonusing and bounty arrangements for private firms, there was an expansion in the manufacturing sector, particularly in Central Canada. The wave of prosperity may have been associated in people's minds with the tariffs, but much of it was induced by the railway building boom. In any case, much of the new investment in manufacturing was of a type that brought little comment in its day but has had momentous import for Canada in the twentieth century. A number of the new firms that were being established in Canada in the last two decades of the nineteenth century were branch plants of American firms, expanding to Canada to establish themselves behind the tariff wall or to protect their patents in the Canadian market. This was the early penetration of the multinational corporation, which has now come to dominate the Canadian economy.

Other goals of the national policy were achieved more slowly. Despite the completion of the Pacific railway by 1885, the great promise of the agricultural West was not realized quickly. Immigration, despite government encouragement, was sporadic, much of it in the form of ethnic and religious colonies. World trade was depressed and the European market for grain was weak. The American frontier was still more attractive than the Canadian. Western grievances against the eastern domination increased, particularly against the refusal of the federal government to allow Manitoba to charter railways that would give the region connections with the American market. Also the gradual destruction of the economic base of the native population again prompted rebellion and once again Riel was at the head. This time, however, he was completely unsuccessful and the old way of prairie life died on the battlefield of Batoche in 1885.

British Columbia throughout this period had even more limited contact with eastern Canada. Yet, it also had grievances, particularly the disallowance by Ottawa of provincial legislation to restrict the continuing immigration of Oriental labour to the West Coast, an influx which the provincial government felt was depressing the labour market, particularly in the Vancouver Island coal mines, and producing social discord.

The whole situation in the West was transformed by two major world economic developments. The first was the opening up of the mining frontier in the western mountain states in the U.S. and extending into south-eastern British Columbia. The B.C. mining frontier became tributary to the United States economy, in defiance of the designs of the national policy, because of the lack of Canadian transportation into the region. Once again the CPR became the vehicle of the eastern Canadian empire. In exchange for a large public subsidy, the CPR built the Crow's Nest Pass line, which connected the mining region to the main CPR line at Lethbridge and the southeast B.C. mineral economy was effectively reintegrated into the Canadian economy. As part of the deal with the government, the CPR agreed to lower the rail rates on eastern bound grain from the Prairies and on western bound settlers' effects, supposedly in perpetuity.

At about the same time, the world economy was expanding, ocean freight rates had been dropping dramatically, the American frontier was filled up and European demand for grain increased sharply. Conditions were at last ripe for the opening up of the "last best west" in Canada. From just before the turn of the century the flood of immigration to the Canadian Prairies was on. And if one railway was good, two would be better and three even better still. The Grand Trunk Pacific and its eastern link, the National Transcontinental, and the Canadian Northern began to spread across the country. Laurier's boast that the twentieth century belonged to Canada was a popular manifestation of the prevailing mood. For a little over a decade the people came and the wheat economy expanded.

The woods and valleys of British Columbia provided lumber and fruit for the new homesteads; coal from the Crow's Nest Pass and Alberta fed the steam locomotives, prairie hearths and the smelters of southern B.C.

Manufactures, steel rails, kitchen ranges, farm machinery and binder twine moved west from the factories of Central Canada. Prosperity seemed to be everywhere. Everywhere, that is, except in the Atlantic region. Except for the steel producing region of Nova Scotia, the dreams of Confederation floundered. The seeds of Atlantic stagnation, sown in the national policy, were being harvested by the end of the nineteenth century.

Maritime Stagnation

The maritime provinces were integrated into the Atlantic economy at Confederation. Fish, ships and lumber, the staple trades of the Maritimes, found their prime markets in Britain and the West Indies, and most of the remainder was shipped to the American seaboard. In fact, until 1871 when the Intercolonial Railway was completed, the price the maritime provinces extracted for entering the new nation, the fundamental transportation link between the regions did not exist. The rail connection between the two regions was completed just before world conditions began to undermine the economic base of the lower provinces. The worldwide decline in international trade, resulting from the depression that began in 1873, was just the beginning of the long-term decline in the British-West Indies connection and the ocean shipping by sail that had been the basis of the earlier prosperity. With it went the shipbuilding and carrying trade.

Maritime opinion shifted, as in Central Canada, towards a protectionist policy and spokesmen generally welcomed the National Policy Tariff. The 1880s seemed to prove the wisdom of the new policy as growing industrialism more than compensated for the decline in the traditional Atlantic orientation. Protected from the world glut of sugar, refineries multiplied. Cotton and woolen mills, ropes, glass, metal, lumber and iron and steel manufacturing mushroomed. The industrial expansion of the Maritimes, aided by low and preferential rail rates on goods moving west on the Intercolonial Railway, expanded the fortunes of the merchants-turned-industrialists in the dispersed urban settlements of the Atlantic provinces. The growth even outstripped that of the developing manufacturing centres of Central Canada. But the boom of the early 1880s, fueled by western railway expansion, was short-lived. By the end of the decade, the renewal of depression allowed the longer term trends to re-emerge.

The decline in the Atlantic trade in which the Maritimers held a trade surplus undermined the ability of the region to run a trade deficit with Central Canada, which had replaced British and American sources for manufactured goods and for foodstuffs. The Maritimes had to sell to Central Canada or face decline. In the prosperity of the 1880s it was able to do so. But two factors were now powerfully arrayed against it. One was the overexpansion of manufacturing capacity during the brief years of prosperity in Central Canada, the Atlantic provinces and the United States. The second was a new evolutionary stage in North American industrial capitalism, the merging of smaller competitive firms into the large corporations which dominate the contemporary economy. The two were not unrelated.

Economic downturn brought crisis to overexpanded industry. The only alternative was restriction of supply, the repression of competition. Weaker firms facing bankruptcy were easy prey to takeover by stronger and maritime firms were particularly vulnerable. Their export markets were distant, dependent on the wholesaling houses of Montreal. America was increasingly protectionist and willing to dump excess output on the Canadian market. Financial backing for east coast firms was dependent on local sources, both private fortunes and the commercial banks. There was no local stock market to provide the capital and absorb the risks.

Close to a bigger market, with intimate connections with the wholesale distributors and access to the Montreal stock market, the finance capitalists of Central Canada (among them a maritime expatriate, Max Aitken) consolidated and centralized control. By 1895, the Maritimes had lost control of their industry except for part of the iron and steel industry and much of the staple-related processing. Even in the coal industry, CPR-backed interests had taken control through vertical integration to protect themselves from the threat of instability from American competition.

Atlantic manufacturing had become a branch plant of Montreal. It was only a matter of time — two decades — before the iron and steel industry also passed to Central Canadian control. Deindustrialization had begun. The decentralized structure of the area, based on its maritime commercial orientation had succumbed to the centralized continental orientation of Montreal and Toronto. The region's great financial houses, built on the profits of the West Indies' trades, slipped inexorably from the Atlantic periphery to the centre of action, the St. Lawrence metropoles of Central Canada, Montreal and Toronto.

If the twentieth century belonged to Canada, the period of possession was very brief. The integration of the various regions of Canada that had been the goal of the national policy had already begun to fall into disarray in the Maritimes by the turn of the century and was further set back by the First World War. By the depression of the 1930s, the national policy was a dead letter, the national economy was in complete collapse and regional integration was a fast fading memory.

National Economic Disintegration

The trans-Canada boom that resulted from the expansion of the western agricultural frontier and the construction of the two transcontinental railways and the branch lines feeding them — the grain handling system of loading platforms, elevators and terminals, the myriad of towns that provided the stores, the hotels, the transportation connections and all the other services that were required for a widely dispersed rural population — had reached its limits. The integration of the Canadian economy had been based very heavily on providing settler goods and investment capital for the extension of the wheat economy. The end of the growth phase meant a very substantial weakening of the east-west link in the Canadian economy. One result was the revival of depression in Canada even before the First World War, in 1912. The effects of the war temporarily relieved the economic distress but the ultimate effect was to further weaken Canadian economic unity.

Wartime economic demands at first masked the decline in national integration. The use of Atlantic ports and the demand for iron and steel for the military effort offset the decline in demand for railway rails from the Maritimes; in fact, the metal industries in all regions were extended by munitions demands. The prime beneficiary, however, was Ontario, where the existing concentration of metal fabrication was strengthened on the lucrative profits of war contracts. Ontario's manufacturing advantage was consolidated in time to take advantage of the postwar expansion in a whole new range of consumer goods, particularly the automobile and electrical products.

Incompetent financing of the greatly increased demands of the war effort contributed to substantial inflation across the country, that, with war profiteering, helped increase the concentration of wealth. But it also contributed to the destruction of the transportation policy that had provided some measure of protection to the east coast region.

Two transcontinental railways in Canada might have been possible to justify, but three was ridiculous. Nevertheless, because of the enormous profits to be made by railway promoters (with minimal risks to themselves and maximum risks to the public), and the ineptness of Prime Minister Laurier's railway policy, Canada had three railways by the outbreak of the First World War. Prewar depression, the decline in rail traffic and immigration, the withdrawal of the British from the financial markets and the inflation in operating costs all contributed to bringing the two newest railways to the verge of bankruptcy. The government was forced to intercede in 1918, nationalizing the inefficient private systems and integrating them with the already publically owned and economically efficient Intercolonial into one system, the Canadian National Railway (CNR). Until then, the Intercolonial, recognizing the competitive difficulties of maritime manufacturing, had instituted a preferential rate on traffic moving westward. This enabled the region to maintain some advantage in the national market created by Confederation.

Opposition to this rate structure had come from industrialists in Central Canada and also from the far West, where the rate structure discriminated against them. The new CNR management responded not only by removing the preferential rate but also by moving the administrative headquarters and staff of the Intercolonial from the Maritimes to Toronto. Centralization triumphed again over the hinterland regions. Ironically, the effect was to turn profits to losses on the Intercolonial, further burdening the Canadian taxpayer with the inefficiencies of private enterprise.

The effects were immediate. The profitability of manufacturing in the Maritimes for westward export dropped appreciably just at the time when these industries should have been converting back from wartime munitions production to peacetime products. Reduced profits and higher costs contributed to a collapse of investment. Combined with the postwar depression and changes in the structure of the economy, maritime manufacturing employment declined by over 40 per cent from 1917 to 1921 and even later in the decade when the national economy reached its economic peak, the region's industrial employment never reached anywhere near the level of employment at the end of the war. After repeated protestations and threats to pull out of Confederation, and more importantly, the election of a minority government, a Royal Commission was appointed. As a result of its recommendations, the Maritime Freight Rates Act, which went part way to restoring the preferential rates the Maritimers had previously enjoyed, was passed in 1927.

But it was too little, too late. The downward spiral of industry in the region could not be stopped, particularly since the rise of road and truck transportation made even the partial restoration of preferential railway rates largely meaningless.

Western Regionalism

The western region fared little better except that, in its case, railway rate policy had never favoured industry in the region. Federal policy accepted that once the centrally controlled CPR was constructed, it should operate at a profit and the West could absorb the costs of operating the unprofitable sections north of the Great Lakes and through the Rockies. The monopoly the CPR enjoyed for many years in the West meant that it could pass these costs on, whereas in Central Canada, competitive railways and water transport held down the rates. This was why the Manitoba government was so insistent on chartering a competitive line connecting with the American railway system — and why the federal government was equally insistent on disallowing such legislation. Although the federal government finally gave in in 1888 (in exchange for more financial aid in the form of a bond guarantee to the CPR, which needed working capital), Westerners found the American railways almost equally determined to charge what the traffic would bear, and a new railroad was never built.

The Crow's Nest Pass agreement in 1897 lowered rates for export grains and for imported settlers' effects; and without doubt gave a strong impetus for the expansion of western agriculture. It also encouraged extreme specialization on the Prairies by lowering the costs of exporting wheat, and at the same time, lowered the cost of importing manufactured goods, thereby discouraging investment in regionally based manufacturing. B.C. did not benefit because the preferences applied only to westbound goods. The prairie provinces became the private preserve of central Canadian industry. Winnipeg benefited for a while by becoming the satellite merchant distribution centre, a role that Montreal was increasingly filling for the Quebec and maritime hinterlands.

The First World War brought an end to the preferential railway rates for the Prairies as well as for the Maritimes. Western protestations were even more vociferous, manifested in the election of a large contingent of the Progressive party to a federal minority parliament. The final result was again a compromise. The lower Crow's Nest Pass rates of export grain were reintroduced by statute in 1925 but the lower rates for west-bound goods were abandoned permanently. In any case, by then, Central Canada had such an advantage in manufacturing that the protective effect of higher rates on west-bound traffic did little to encourage economic diversification.

The extension of Crow's Nest Pass rates to east- and west-bound grains and more recently to vegetable oil seeds means it is much cheaper to ship out raw products than it is to ship out processed or manufactured products. The statutory rates have come to be a cosy tariff barrier protecting eastern processors against western competition, thus increasing the dependency of the region on primary production. Just as improved transportation by way of the railways "appears to have been more successful in opening the Maritime market to Central Canada than in opening the Ontario and Quebec markets to the Maritime Provinces", the transcontinental railways opened the western region to eastern Canada, but did not open eastern Canada to the West.

Western regional discontent was not restricted to concern over transport rates. Another major source of discontent was the monopoly control of the grainhandling system, in the coalition of the CPR with the central Canadian-controlled milling companies and grain handling system. The other was the tariff. Although the tariff was in place before the West was settled, it became — and remains — a source of grievance to the western region. The cry of raw producers in the West has long been "Why must we buy on a high cost market protected by tariffs and sell on an unstable, unprotected world market?" Laurier heard the cry when he came west, desperately seeking support before the 1911 election. He adopted reciprocal free trade with the U.S. as a campaign slogan, to no avail. Thirty years of protection had created strong vested interests in Central Canada, whose numbers crushed the protesting voice of the resource hinterland.

The battle was renewed after the war by the Progressive Party and other western farmer-labour groups. The one major and lasting result was the wheat pools, which were grain handling and marketing cooperatives. A significant portion of the wheat handling system had come under regional control, just in time to take the full brunt of the worldwide collapse in grain markets and the natural climatic catastrophe, the great drought. It was also the time when the federal government formally abandoned the national policy by restoring to the provincial governments what was left after all the land grants of the prairie lands. At that time little was known of the mineral and petroleum resources that lay below the land, which were to later change the face of the region.

The Harvest of Dependence

The spectacular growth and expansion of the wheat economy in the early years of the century overshadowed the beginnings of a structural change in the Canadian economy that was to reinforce regional divisions and further reduce Canadian economic integration. Even before the First World War, the raw material, staple industries were expanding as resource hinterlands to the American market. Pulp and paper, mining and hydroelectricity were expanding in the infertile, non-settled frontier of the Maritimes, Quebec, Ontario and British Columbia. But unlike the agricultural frontier before it, or even the earlier precious metal frontier in southeastern B.C., the effect of these new industries did little to develop or integrate the Canadian economy. The main effect was to create pockets of development in otherwise underdeveloped subregions. More seriously for Canadian nationhood, these pockets maintained an almost independent existence from the east-west economy that the national policy had, at great expense and effort, created.

The reasons are very simple. The markets were largely American. The capital was largely American. Geographically, the location was far from existing urban and rural settlement. Though the average wages paid were respectable, and improved as the degree of unionization increased in later years, the industries were users of large amounts of capital, not of labour and did little to stem the tide of outmigration from areas like the Maritimes where, for example, outmigration in the first three decades of this century was about 100 times greater than employment in the pulp and paper industry.

Mining was heavily concentrated in isolated centres in Ontario and B.C. and the number of smelters and refineries in the whole nation was generally less than ten, and even much less if we consider only the significant ones. It was a case of enclave economies within but largely unrelated to the Canadian economy, which in the Maritimes or B.C. had scarcely any connections with the older centres of Halifax, St. John or Vancouver, except to the extent that taxes or royalties might feed the provincial coffers. In this period of ultra-conservative government, even this benefit was small. Providing public services like education and transportation might cost more than these industries were worth.

The benefits to Central Canada were scarcely better, but the major cities of Central Canada had acquired two essential functions that reaped them much greater benefits than the cities of the hinterland regions. The heritage of the national policy had concentrated manufacturing in Central Canada, more specifically, in Ontario. The following table gives some idea of this degree of concentration.

Table 3-1

REGIONAL CONCENTRATION OF CANADIAN NET PRODUCTION IN SELECTED MANUFACTURING INDUSTRIES 1929

Industry	Ont. %	Que. %	Rest of Canada %
Pulp and Paper	32	54	14
Non-ferrous metals smelting	55	23	22
Central Electric stations	42	33	25
Electrical Apparatus and supply	77	22	1
Automobiles	96	—	4
Rubber tires, etc.	95	4	1
Machinery	72	25	3
Casting and Forgings	69	21	10
Railway rolling stock	23	53	24
Hardware and Tools	68	29	3
Agricultural Implements	95	3	2
Cigars and Cigarettes	14	86	—
Cotton Yarn and Cloth	18	75	7
Boots and shoes	36	60	4
Rubber footwear	38	62	—
Clothing, men's	36	61	3
Clothing, women's	56	40	4
Hosiery and Knit goods	72	22	6
Furniture and upholstery	76	18	6
All Manufacture	51	31	18

Consumer demand in the resource settlements might be limited by the relatively small number of people involved, but what did occur would accrue to the benefit of the industrialized subregion of Central Canada.

Toronto and Montreal also benefited because of the concentration of financial markets and commercial services in their environs. Despite the head start that Montreal might have had in this function, the fact that its economic connections were with the St. Lawrence system rather than its Quebec hinterland, shifted the centre of this activity west, a factor in its steady loss of importance relative to Toronto. Concentration fosters further concentration.

The figures in the above table, however, reveal an even more pronounced process of regionalization than the preceding narrative has suggested. The 1920s was the decade when a new era of durable consumer goods based on electricity and the automobile emerged. In the age of the gasoline engine, 96 per cent of the Canadian output of automobiles, 95 per cent of rubber tires, 95 per cent of agricultural implements, 72 per cent of machinery and 68 per cent of hardware and tools was from Ontario. On the other hand, as railways declined in relative importance, 53 per cent of rolling stock was produced in Quebec and 24 per cent in the hinterland regions, largely Nova Scotia and Manitoba. With the new era of electrical goods, 77 per cent of the Canadian output of electrical apparatus and supplies were produced in Ontario, almost double that province's share of electrical power generation. In the older, traditional slow growth, light, nondurable industries, Quebec was dominant; it produced 86 per cent of Canada's cigars and cigarettes, 75 per cent of its cotton, 60 per cent of boots and shoes, 62 per cent of rubber footwear, 61 per cent of men's clothing, and so on. The stamp of regional disparities was indelibly imprinted even before the great depression of the 1930s. The depression only intensified them.

A half century of the national policy had produced a

national economy in name only. True, the St. Lawrence heartland, thanks to the protective tariff, served the nation for manufactures even if increasingly those manufactures were the product of American branch plants, moved a few miles across the international border to take advantage of the Canadian tariff and the British Empire market in which Canadian products had preference. Outside of this heartland, the regions were resource hinterlands, dependent on European markets for cereals and pulp and paper or American markets for increasing amounts of many natural resources to augment her diminishing supplies, and on American capital to develop these resources.

The Depression

The harvest of this dependency was reaped in the grim decade of the 1930s. Whatever the cause of this debacle of the capitalist world, the prime manifestation was a collapse of international trade and with it, investment. The result was massive unemployment and deprivation. Regions that were dependent on primary exports were naturally the most seriously affected. Not only did their markets disappear, but with them went any hope of investment expenditure in the resource industries. Labour was unemployed, but so also were the mines and smelters, the mills and refineries that readied the resources for export. The construction industries suffered accordingly. Canadian government policy merely added to the distress of the export-dependent regions.

Two policy measures, taken together, illustrate the regional inequality of federal policy. The first was the attempt to maintain the value of the Canadian dollar in terms of its gold value while all the competitive exporting countries let their money values fall. This meant, for instance, that Canadian farmers who wanted to sell their grain had to match the international price by lowering their farm price, not only to compensate for the fall in real prices, but also to compensate for the rising price in international markets of the Canadian dollar. This was a double burden. For the first four years of the depression, the Canadian dollar remained overvalued for the sake of those who believed in the "sound dollar". Why? Because to devalue the dollar would increase the burden of debt of the nation which had been heavily financed in foreign countries.

The Saskatchewan brief to the Royal Commission on Dominion-Provincial Relations a few years later made it clear that the West was well aware of the burden placed on the export-based regions:

> The western farmer made a sacrifice for the rest of Canada, but a sacrifice that brought distressing results upon him. Many westerners are not free of the belief that such sacrifices are frequently called for as a result of the centralization of power in eastern Canada.

The same is true of any resource export region in Canada facing a competitive international market.

If other policies had been left unchanged, the manufacturing interests would also have been adversely affected by the upward valuation of the dollar. Imported goods would have become much cheaper and replaced Canadian produced goods. However, a sharp upward revision of the tariffs offset the high value of the dollar and further depressed the exporting regions. Foreign goods were kept out and demand was diverted to home production, that is, to Central Canada. With export industries growing and income expanding, the diversion of purchasing power to protected home industries would be borne, if not always with equanimity. In periods of economic collapse, with income falling and unemployment rising, the added regional burden was intolerable.

By the mid-thirties, the value of the Canadian dollar had been allowed to fall. Negotiations had begun with the United States to reduce tariff protection between the two countries. But by then the drought had wrecked further havoc throughout the Prairies. Saskatchewan was particularly badly hit. Economics and nature had conspired to reduce the province to abject poverty. Between 1928 and 1933 provincial income fell by over 70 per cent. In 1933 federal relief expenditures in the province, grossly inadequate as they were, still made up 5 per cent of the total provincial income.

British Columbia, with its heavy dependence on export resources, was also devastated by the depression. The provincial income decreased more than 40 per cent between 1929 and 1933 while wages and salaries declined almost 50 per cent. B.C. would have suffered more and longer but because of the lumber preferences which were negotiated in the 1932 Ottawa agreement with Britain, lumber exports began a sharp recovery in that year.

The greater the dependence of the provincial or regional economies on exports of resources and agricultural markets, the more severe was the economic collapse. When recovery began for the mining industry, much of the expansionary effect in these export regions was lost because profits and investment income, which rose first, were exported from the regions, due to the very high degree of foreign ownership. The regions suffered from a dual dependency on foreign markets and foreign capital.

Summary

The Canadian nation was founded on a regional specialization plan. Established centres of Central Canada and of the Maritimes were to provide the manufactures for the resource-specialized West and peripheral regions in the Canadian Shield. East and West were to be linked by a railway and the link protected by high tariffs. But the great dream of the St. Lawrence developers began to come unstuck almost from its inception. The Maritimes deindustrialized, the victim of the tendency in capitalist economies to regional concentration when once the peripheral areas are opened by the railway to continental influence. All markets in all regions were increasingly filled by products from the American branch plants of the rising oligopolies which had slipped across the border to settle behind the tariff wall.

The West was filled, and for a brief period the whole national economy was buoyed by the development expenditure. But the boom was short-lived. By the 1920s the new frontiers were in the minerals and woods of the Canadian Shield and B.C., almost totally dependent on (mainly American) foreign markets and foreign capital. The collapse of exports in the depression, therefore, provided dramatic evidence of the vulnerability of dependent economies. The regional inequalities that were part of Canada's development strategy were likewise intensified by that development policy.

In the face of the catastrophic depression, the federal government responded in its usual way, by appointing a Royal Commission. But just as the report on Dominion-Provincial Relations, better known as the Rowell-Sirois Commission, was readied, war broke out, again rescuing North American capitalism, and with it, the Canadian resource regions.

Since the war, little has fundamentally changed; the trends of the 1920s have only been intensified. Canadian dependence on American capital has increased along with its dependence on continental resource markets. Regions rich in natural resources have fared well, if one uses as measures provincial growth rates, wage levels and, in some cases, provincial government income from resource royalties. But for much of the country, employment generation has been modest or poor, unable to absorb the rural outflow and the natural increase in population: the Maritimes, underendowed with resources now in demand, have continued their stagnation that began 80 years ago.

4
The Continuing Failure of Liberal Economics

After the [Second World] War, we were well placed to have the [wartime] stimulus continued by American investment. Such capital was an irresistible substitute for wartime government spending, and we made ourselves extraordinarily open to it. Reacting from the painful restrictionism of the 1930s we did not allow our enthusiasm for lower tariffs and trade expansion to be curbed by the fact that in practice it meant a massive expansion only in trade with the United States.

Thus we had at last a Canadian economic policy different from the old national policy. It could hardly have been more different. It gave us what I called at the time, the American boom in Canada. Unlike the national policy, it was short-lived. It faded out after 1956, for lack of a continuing political consensus behind the policy. But like the old policy, it has not been replaced by any clear substitute. What we have had, for 18 years now, is incoherence in national economic policy.

The depression of the 1930s brought the national policy vision of integrated regional economies to an end and brought the extreme vulnerability of the Canadian economy (and of the western region in particular), to the attention of policy-makers. The Canadian government was forced to act in the face of regional calamity and the Wheat Board was reluctantly established in an attempt to rescue the prairie farmer. Conservative Prime Minister

R.B. Bennett made his death-bed preelection repentance in 1935 through his legislation to establish the partial foundations of a welfare state — to no electoral or judicial avail. Bennett lost the election and the legislation was declared *ultra vires* by the courts.

But the depression did provoke the first true re-examination of Confederation and economic regional disparities with the appointment of the Rowell-Sirois Royal Commission on Dominion-Provincial Relations. The Commission report was completed just in time to be overshadowed by the outbreak of the Second World War, which solved the immediate problem of economic depression. Federal government power was temporarily increased with wartime emergency provisions. Unemployment insurance was enacted through a constitutional change and the family allowance program was inaugurated. The demands of war solved the immediate cyclical problem but not the long term structural one. Through the halcyon days of the postwar boom, regional inequality took a back seat to growth — until the boom came to an end in the mid-1950s and the old problems once more came to the forefront. It was Quebec's "quiet revolution" of the sixties that turned governments, federal and provincial, to the question of regional development. This is the story of the failure of those government policies to tackle this question successfully.

The Origins of Postwar Policy

Regional assistance programs are not new in Canada. Even if we exclude the development type of expenditures that characterized the first half century of Confederation, the great depression of the 1930s forced a reluctant federal government to intercede with aid to bankrupt provincial administrations, particularly in western Canada. Across the country, federal relief expenditures and advances approached a billion dollars. One province, devastated Saskatchewan, received $140 million in federal relief by 1938. But these transfers were only an emergency response to a crisis. Nevertheless, they prompted one of the early and systematic stabilization programs, the Prairie Farm Rehabilitation Act (PFRA) of 1935 which was designed to conserve and develop water supplies and rehabilitate land in the drought-ridden west. There was also the Prairie Farm Assistance Act of 1939, a primitive and rather limited form of farm income insurance.

The real impetus for regional development and assistance programs, however, did not come until after the war and reflected the spirit, if not the letter, of the recommendations of the Rowell-Sirois Commission. The Commission's cautious spirit is reflected in its report:

> When as a result of national policies undertaken in the general interest, one region or class or individual is fortuitously enriched and others impoverished, it would appear that there is some obligation, if not to redress the balance, at least to provide for the victim.

But the federal government, largely as a result of questionable judicial interpretation of the distribution of powers in the BNA Act, was unable to do this directly. The form which it finally took in the 1956 federal-provincial tax sharing agreement, and which has been maintained since, is the tax equalization payment. Under this agreement the federal government transmits to the provinces unconditional grants sufficient to bring per capita tax revenues in the poorer provinces up to the average per capita level of standard taxes in the two richest provinces. Although the details have changed since 1956, the principle of equalization grants remains.

In 1974-75 equalization payments amounted to $1.8 billion. Newfoundland and P.E.I. received about $350 per person, Nova Scotia and New Brunswick about $275, Quebec $160, Manitoba and Saskatchewan between $100 and $150. The "have provinces", Ontario, Alberta and British Columbia, did not receive any equalization. Nor did the Yukon or Northwest Territories, which are financed directly by Ottawa.

Equalization grants obviously go some way toward

providing at least the public sector with a degree of income redistribution and equality. But it is obvious that while the grants may alleviate some problems of public finance, they have done little to reduce regional disparities. If the Economic Council's estimates are correct, average personal income in Newfoundland and P.E.I. would be $400 to $500 lower if federal transfers were eliminated, while Ontario's and Alberta's would be a little more than $100 higher.

Despite the transfers to the poorer provinces, regional disparities have not declined appreciably. During the 1960s, rising Quebec nationalism and the aroused concern with economic growth throughout the country (prompted by the American "war on poverty") prodded Ottawa to explore numerous additional avenues for stimulating regional growth. The pendulum swung from merely compensating poorer provinces for their limited tax bases to actively promoting economic activity in problem areas.

The first such aggressive program was the Agricultural Rehabilitation and Development Act, passed in 1961. Its goals were similar to if more comprehensive than the PFRA, 25 years its senior: to conserve water and improve land and to redirect marginal land into its most economically efficient use. Its approach progressively broadened to encompass more comprehensive schemes of rural development, including much more than just farm improvement. In 1965 the broadened scope was recognized in a new name, the Agricultural and Rural Development Act. But even this expanded program was insufficient for the magnitude of adjustment problems caused by rural decline. In 1966 the Fund for Rural Economic Development (FRED) was created with the recognition that adjustments to agricultural resources were insufficient. The FRED mandate essentially provided for agricultural change, the funding of infrastructure (education, transportation facilities and social and economic support services) and industrial development. As such it comprised a more substantial attack on regional rural poverty.

The government assault on disparities was not restricted to rural areas. The Atlantic Development Board was established in 1962 and was given a fund of $100 million to promote a comprehensive development plan and attract industry for the Maritimes. The following year the Area Development Act was passed to provide for tax and depreciation concessions for industries locating in problem regions. In 1965, the passage of the Area Development Incentives Act provided capital grants as well as tax incentives to induce industry to locate in designated poorer regions.

This haphazard evolution of regional programs reflects the gradual realization by the politicians and bureaucracy in Ottawa that the postwar boom in Canada, set off by the expansion of the American economy, was producing uneven, unbalanced growth and that the Maritimes, the Prairies and Quebec were growing dissatisfied with the results of the laissez-faire approach to economic growth in the country.

Ottawa abandoned its ad hoc approach with the creation of the Department of Regional Economic Expansion (DREE) in 1969.* Between 1970 and 1973, the new department singled out 23 "special areas" for development attention and provided a budget of $680 million for grant-loan assistance. By 1975, $254 million had been paid out in grants under the Regional Development Incentives Act. All in all, by 1975 a total of over one and a half billion dollars was spent, 45 per cent in the Atlantic region, 35 per cent in Quebec, 12 per cent in the Prairies, 6 per cent in Ontario and 2 per cent in B.C.

* There were also a number of other regional programs in effect in 1969, of greater or lesser importance, that were incorporated into or under DREE — the Canada Land Inventory, the Newfoundland Resettlement Program, the Maritime Marshland Rehabilitation Act, the Atlantic Provinces Power Development Act, the New Start program, the Cape Breton Development Corporation and the Canadian Council on Rural Development.

Table 4-1

DREE EXPENDITURE PER CAPITA, GRANTS AND CONTRIBUTIONS: 1969-75

Newfoundland	352
P.E.I.	807
Nova Scotia	230
New Brunswick	386
Quebec	86
Ontario	13
Manitoba	91
Saskatchewan	38
Alberta	40
British Columbia	15

In spite of all this activity and expenditure, DREE itself concluded: "The programs were not in themselves enough to alter the trend toward increased economic activity in the industrial heartland of the country." The program had, by and large, been a billion and a half dollar failure. How much worse disparities might have become without the program is difficult to say.

The DREE approach, with its controversial component of "corporate welfare" (capital subsidies through incentive grants) was not the only federal line of attack on the problem of declining regions. Many economists argue that if capital will not move to labour, then labour should be moved to capital. In practice this means depopulate the Maritimes, Quebec and the Prairies in favour of southern Ontario, British Columbia and Alberta. The Department of Manpower and Immigration was created in 1966 to take over the Manpower and Mobility Program initiated the previous year and it provided grants to workers from high unemployment areas willing to relocate in areas of low unemployment.

The record of labour migration in diminishing disparities has been barely more successful than the capital incentive schemes. Between 1951 and 1971 a net outmigration of 15 per cent of the population of the Atlantic region did nothing to reduce the gap between the region's unemployment rate and that of the Canadian average. Federal expenditures on relocation grants worth in the neighbourhood of $25 million by 1976, have proved to be little use in lessening unemployment disparities even though they may have lightened the dislocation costs of the individual migrant. In any case, the generally depressed state of the Canadian economy means that there are few low unemployment areas to which labour can move.

These schemes do not exhaust all of the transfers initiated by the federal government to shore up not only the poorer regions but the whole economy. The size of the federal presence is indicated in the following table.

Table 4-2

FEDERAL GRANTS, CONTRIBUTIONS AND TRANSFERS: DOLLARS PER CAPITA, 1974-75

	Atlantic	*Que.*	*Ont.*	*Prairies*	*B.C.*	*Canada*
Grants to Business	23	33	23	40	17	28
Transfers to Individuals*	537	408	284	362	466	410
(Unemployment Ins.)	(169)	(131)	(84)	(43)	(131)	(103)
Total Transfers	560	441	307	402	483	439

> * Includes Unemployment Insurance, Old Age, Veterans and other pensions, family allowances, manpower allowances and miscellaneous transfers.

Except for the old age pension and guaranteed income supplement, the biggest transfer is for unemployment insurance, a stark reminder of the costs of unemployment, particularly in the depressed regions.

It is not difficult to understand what precipitated the federal move into regional development. The growing sentiment for Quebec independence was rooted in the stunted development and lack of opportunity in the

French-speaking community. But the lack of any appreciable success by Ottawa in closing regional disparities or in stemming separatist sentiment should not be taken to mean that there have been no positive benefits. The creation of DREE has greatly reduced the competitive giveaways by provinces and municipalities that were characteristic of interprovincial attempts to attract industry and jobs.

Provincial Reactions

Provincial governments in Canada have not been ready to accept the inevitable hinterland status that successive federal governments have been willing to accede to. They question why there should be depressed regions in a rich and high income economy. But the iron law of uneven development in capitalist economies has made it impossible for them to promote industrial growth. Almost every provincial government outside of the main manufacturing belt has tried to institute the big development project that would herald the end of dependent growth. But the results have been a succession of failures. Financial journalist Philip Mathias in his book *Forced Growth* documents a number of these failures.

The basic motivation common to these attempts at economic stimulation was to overcome regional disparities. They occurred in the poorer provinces where provincial governments, faced with a lack of industrial growth, lagging employment, outmigration of younger workers and stagnant or declining population and depressed or declining traditional industries, opened the public purse to facilitate private developments in an almost desperate attempt to spur new growth.

One of Mathias' case studies is a P.E.I. fish processing plant, Georgetown Seafoods Ltd., which produced its first output in 1965. P.E.I., plagued by high unemployment (15 per cent or more in the slow winter months) and the declining ability of agriculture (the province's major resource), to absorb the natural population growth,

entered into financial agreements with a private pro-
moter to support a fish plant and a subsidiary shipyard to
build fishing trawlers. After a history of inept governmental dealings with the promoters, both companies
were insolvent and the province was left with a debt of
over $9 million for companies that were worth perhaps
around $3 million.

Newfoundland fared better with its dealings with the
Churchill Falls Hydro project in Labrador. No government money was initially expended although huge resource concessions were offered to the British-controlled
multinational, BRINCO, that ultimately built the massive project. In exchange, the province was to receive
$15 million or so annually. But in 1974, Newfoundland
nationalized the hydro project for $160 million, leaving
BRINCO with the mineral rights. However, the hydro
power produced is almost all exported to Quebec and the
United States while in Newfoundland, electricity for provincial needs is generated by much more expensive ther-
mal plants. As the *Financial Post* noted, "Alas, today the
Churchill Falls power plant is tied to a 65-year contract to
provide Quebec with $500 million worth of saleable hy-
dro a year, leaving Newfoundland with hardly enough
money to amortize the debt."

Although Newfoundland fared relatively well in the
Churchill Falls venture, it came off disastrously in its
other efforts at this type of development scheme, as the
recent abandonment of the Labrador Linerboard plant,
or the bankruptcy of the Come-by-Chance refinery have
demonstrated. Between the two, the province has been
left with debts of $250 million.

Both Nova Scotia and New Brunswick have made val-
iant development attempts — Nova Scotia with its heavy
water plant, New Brunswick with its Bricklin sports car.
In both cases, the provinces were drawn into financial
involvement by entrepreneurs, who were promoting
their own technical innovations. Both went wrong for
technical and managerial reasons, leaving Nova Scotia

with an inoperable heavy water plant for which it had paid $150 million and New Brunswick with a bankrupt plant and a loss of $23 million. The *Financial Post* noted the New Brunswick Premier's reaction at the time: "Part of the problem was the attitude in Central Canada that we should stick with our resources. We couldn't even get a licence to sell in Canada until the thing was practically dead!" The experience in Manitoba would tend to support this position. Federal government support for Manitoba's Saunders Aircraft was non-existent despite the fact that the aircraft appeared to be an engineering and, potentially, an economic success.

Saskatchewan attempted to diversify its economic base from dependence on wheat and potash, both of which were in a depressed condition in the late 1960s, by entering into an agreement with an American company, Parsons and Whittemore, to build two pulp mills, at Prince Albert and Meadow Lake. While the province absorbed most of the financial risk as well as providing subsidized pulp wood and roads and other assistance, it received only a small part of the equity in the two plants. The people of Saskatchewan paid a high price — about $180,000 — for the benefits of a couple of thousand jobs.

Yet the cost of the Saskatchewan pulp mills is no match for the pulp mill debacle in Manitoba concerning Churchill Forest Industries (Manitoba) Ltd. The project was initiated in 1966 by the Conservative government to provide employment growth for northern Manitoba. Although several well-established international companies had shown interest in the plan, the Roblin government chose to back a rather mysterious group of Swiss promoters whose track record was virtually impossible to determine (and the government made no attempt to do so). All of the monies for the project were put up by governments in one form or another, most of it through loans from the Manitoba Development Fund. Control of expenditure was virtually non-existent although some of the blame lay with the government's private consultants. Excessive fees and commissions were funnelled off to secret Swiss bank accounts and by the time a hesitant NDP government had the project placed into receivership in 1971, the province had contracted debts of $100 million or more for a small, inefficient pulp mill complex worth about $60 million. This did not include the other grants and subsidies for roads and community services provided by all levels of government, or the million or so spent by the Inquiry Commission which was established to unravel the tangled web of front companies that had participated in the costly promotion — all for the sake of about 1,400 jobs.

Perhaps none of these problem "developments" was quite so expensive as the sellout of Canadian power resources to American interests involved in B.C.'s Columbia River Treaty, which was acceded to by the federal government in the early 1960s. The cost to Canadians, with little obvious benefit (except perhaps some immediate, if short-lived, political credits to W.A.C. Bennett's Social Credit regime for the development of the Peace River power) has been estimated at up to $600 million.

This chronology of economic misadventures by provincial governments in the 1960s is not intended to demonstrate the incompetence of provincial administrations, although it certainly does so. Nor does it say anything about the efficacy of public enterprise in economic development. All of the projects were initiated by private enterprise governments and were carried out (or not carried out in many cases) by private firms and promoters. What this depressing list of failures shows is the desperation with which provincial governments in the hinterland regions of Canada attempted to cash in on the economic growth of the 1960s that was passing them by.

The basis of the problem is the alienation of the depressed provinces from industrialized Ontario. If the federal government was not willing or able to do anything, the provincial governments were not prepared to sit idly by; and it is this that prompted most of them to establish provincial investment funds and agencies during the 1960s. But lacking any coherent regional strategy from Ottawa, little could be done either through provincial efforts or through Ottawa's own agency, DREE. As Tom Kent concluded, "DREE cannot be expected to plan good regional development strategies unless there is a national industrial strategy of which regional programs are part and with which they can be coordinated. We do not have such a strategy." Neither could the provinces be expected to come up with viable development strategies.

A New Dawn?

The overall failure of federal and provincial programs to promote any significant measure of regional development might appear to be contradicted by recent events in the West, particularly in Alberta. The 1977 *Financial Post*'s *Report* was entitled "The West Takes Off" and was filled with articles such as "Western Wonderland". Has there been a change in national economics that would challenge the pessimistic view based on historical evidence? The example of Alberta would certainly suggest so. Contrary to results in other provinces where the harnessing of major export resource exploitation as the vehicle for economic development is largely under multinational control, Alberta seems to have achieved a large degree of success on its own. It has amassed a huge investment fund, the Heritage Fund, estimated to contain $3.2 billion in March 1978. A petrochemical industry has developed and a strong and aggressive local business class has emerged. The province has bought its own airline, has interests in steel making and in an energy conglomerate with investments in gas, coal and pipelines; and has made its own contribution to national unity by becoming creditor for two Atlantic provinces. Is there a lesson in this for other Canadian hinterland regions?

There is, of course, one obvious lesson — find oil. But there is more to it than that. One dimension is revealed in a comment by Robert Blair, President of Alberta Gas Trunk Ltd. and driving force behind the Alcan Pipeline, about Quebec's economic woes — he states that what is wrong is that Quebec is "full of subsidiaries". What he means is that indigenous development requires local entrepreneurship. A similar point was made by Robert Collison writing on the current Canadian economic crisis: "Foreign managers have little incentive to develop genuinely autonomous industrial capacity in their hinterland Canadian operations." Alberta has been able to develop a domestic entrepreneurial class out of its oil industry. But it has taken several decades and the oil industry has many sectors in which independent operators could get a piece of the action. Large profits and low taxes have permitted the accumulation of private fortunes that are the basis of this new entrepreneurial class.

Also, one of the leading actors in the province's entrepreneurship has been the Alberta government, which has led the way by expropriating a good part of the economic rent (that is, the difference between the world price and the cost of production) from oil and gas. In January 1977, Alberta captured 40 per cent of the $9.75 selling price of a barrel of oil, or $3.90 per barrel. This amounts to an enormous income (in 1977-78 estimated at around $3 billion), 30 per cent of which is paid into the Heritage Fund, the rest to general government revenues. This has provided the funds for its entrepreneurship.

In its recent dealings with Syncrude, the consortium put together to exploit the tar sands, one economist has estimated that Alberta gained a profit of $358 million — at the expense of Ottawa and Ontario. Despite its conservative name, Alberta's government has been aggressive in expanding the province's economic base. However, the Heritage Fund has not been used for risk investment outside of about $35 million invested in irrigation, reclamation and reforestation. Alberta has loaned Newfoundland and New Brunswick $97 million but the rest has been invested in safe bonds and securities, which makes it, as one commentator observed, "the world's largest savings account".

Saskatchewan has also attempted to broaden its base through public entrepreneurship, primarily with the nationalization of a large proportion (approximately half) of its potash industry with revenues from its much more limited oil industry, making the provincially-owned corporation the largest potash producer in the western world. But potash is not oil. Its market is much more unstable, tied to the fortunes of agriculture, and the number of industries that can be built around it are limited, unlike the petrochemical industry that has brought so many jobs to Alberta. Saskatchewan may find it difficult to maintain stable income from potash because of the international potash cartel, dominated by American firms, that has the controlling share of the western world's market.

Yet in a hinterland economy based essentially on two staples, the Saskatchewan move is a significant attempt to moderate its dependency on fluctuating grain markets and foreign-controlled potash production, and at the same time invest the surplus from a fast disappearing non-renewable resource to provide income and jobs for the future.

In British Columbia, new directions have been much less evident, except in the initiative of the former Barrett government for a significant public presence in the forest products industry, a presence that has not to date been reversed by the new Social Credit administration. What is interesting, notes the *Financial Post*, is that in all these cases in the West (and also in Manitoba, until the Conservative government of Sterling Lyon dismantled and destroyed the development program), despite differences in ideology, "One basic economic rationale is common .... All are trying to raise the level of Canadian control — and especially of *Western* Canadian control — of their economies."

Prince Edward Island — A Different Approach

While new directions based on strategies of harnessing resource extraction to economic development seem to be having some measure of success in the West, for resource-poor P.E.I. no such avenue is open. Yet, it too has embarked on a change in policy direction.

Throughout the island's history, agriculture has been the economic base, generating two thirds or more of provincial output. But like agriculture throughout the country, it is in difficulty, caught in the cost-price squeeze. In the decade 1956-66, the number of farms declined by one third and incomes have been low and unstable. In 1969, the provincial and federal governments agreed to a development plan, the basis of which was to increase the efficiency of agriculture and fishing by means of consolidation, thereby creating larger (but fewer) farms and fisheries. Displaced labour was to be absorbed primarily by tourism, an industry that developers often seem to bring to mind when no alternative resource exploitation presents itself. But tourism is a seasonal and, except for resort owners, generally low income employer. It is also unstable, depending on weather and fashion and, as the Canadian tourist operators found to their detriment during the American centenary, highly volatile to outside influences. Other aspects of the development plan, particularly the consolidation of schools, have also been criticized because of the increased bureaucratic costs and loss of local control.

However, Prince Edward Island's provincial administration talks about abandoning the big growth syndrome in favour of a smaller, conserver-type economy. As Premier Alex Campbell, the man who presided over the change in objectives said in 1977: "Ten years ago, five even, I was full of all the buzz words about 'economies of scale', 'infrastructure', 'centralization'. Now it seems to me more and more what Canadians ought to be doing is taking a long and hard look at the essence of our whole society. We have to draw a distinction between the kind of growth that's mostly materialistic and the total human development that a conserver society makes possible."

Prince Edward Island has been, to some extent, propelled into looking at alternatives because of its lack of any natural energy resources and its reliance on imported oil even for electricity generation (although a new submarine cable from New Brunswick will provide a substantial reduction in this dependency on fossil fuels). The result is that the island province has the most expensive electricity in the country. This also explains the directions of the province's Man and Resources Institute, to probe methods of harnessing the energy of sun and wind and to investigate the conversion of electricity generation from oil to wood fired. It has also prompted the Ark project, a largely self-contained experimental living project which uses solar energy and produces a large proportion of its own food. On the more traditional front, the province has been abandoning the big tourist projects for the fishery, the family farm and support for diversification of the province's potato industry. At the same time, emphasis has been placed on enticing and supporting small businesses, from potteries to metal casting of parts for the aerospace industry.

It is too early to evaluate the efficacy of this approach but on a small island largely devoid of natural resources other than land and fish and people, the ultimate judgment may be that there is no other long-term alternative.

Summary

Since the 1920s, Canada has lacked any sort of coherent economic strategy. A number of ad hoc responses to particular crises have developed, and culminated, at the federal level, in the formation of DREE, which, by its own admission, has been largely a failure in combating regional disparities. At the provincial level, the strategies have produced a series of basically disastrous forced growth schemes in the hinterland areas. Saskatchewan and Alberta with their potash and oil riches appear to be moving to newer and more successful provincial strategies, using their resource strength to capitalize industrial development. And tiny and resource-poor P.E.I. has changed direction and strategy in its search for some answers to the perennial disparities problem.

But at the heart of the problem is the lack of any *Canadian* industrial and regional strategy. While the nation's peripheral regions are succumbing to centrifugal forces which are pulling the country apart, the industrial heartland of southern Ontario has increasingly become an appendage of the American continental industrial system. The resource hinterlands are likewise tied to the system — but as "hewers of wood and drawers of water", dependent on metropolitan resource demands. Can Canada break out of this fragmented structure? The answer depends on knowing why disparities seem to persist despite the measures that have been taken. It is necessary to understand the economics of regionalism, the "pathology of disparities".

5
The Economics of Regional Disparities

When Quebec ended a century of passive acceptance of domination by British and American capital in the 1960s, it adopted "maîtres chez nous" — masters of our own house — as its motto. The so-called "quiet revolution" had begun. The election of the Parti Québécois in 1976 was a major step in that same direction. Whether the result will be a separate Quebec depends heavily on whether or not Canada can eliminate regional inequalities in its standard of living and, more important, in economic opportunity. These disparities are a potent source of discontent among French-speaking people in Quebec, and are at least as important as issues of language and culture in the debate about Quebec's future. Moreover, French-speaking Quebecers find that they have to at least compromise, if not abandon their language and culture in seeking equal income and career advancement. The income of French-speaking professionals is substantially lower than the income of their unilingual English-speaking confrères, despite the fact that the province is overwhelmingly French speaking. Pierre Vallières' designation of the French Canadian as a "white nigger" is not far from the truth in economic terms.

But it is not only French-speaking Canadians who face economic dead ends. So do many people in the other dependent regions, although the phenomenon may not be so visible. Maritimers, westerners and northerners often must forsake their home regions to achieve opportunity. The major difference is that, except for the native northerners, they don't have to forsake their language and culture to be part of the system. Canada's version of dependent capitalism decrees centralism and concentration. And centralism breeds further centralism, draining the hinterland regions of vitality, of education, of a financial base and of the resources which could resist economic decline or help develop their own economic potential. This leads to a continuing disadvantage that government grants and transfers may slow down but do not reverse.

Nothing Grows like Growth: Nothing Contracts like Contraction

The pattern of self-perpetuating disparities has been similar in underdeveloped countries and regions elsewhere in the world. Despite the optimistic forecasts of orthodox economists steeped in the world of equilibrium economics, the process of regional disparities has not been self-correcting. Rather it has been cumulative. The history of the Atlantic region is a good example. The decline of the Atlantic trade and the opening of the region to Central Canada weakened the opportunities for the profitable operations of the region's industry. This allowed central Canadian industries with their superior access to financial resources to buy out the local factories, run them down and transfer their markets to centralized factories.

The result in the Maritimes was predictable. The rise in unemployment might very well have contributed to falling wages, which some economists argue should have attracted investment to the region. But instead, falling wages has meant falling buying power. With consumption falling, other industries faced economic troubles. And when the textile mills were shut down, companies which supplied the textile mills with inputs were the victims. The results were falling investment, falling employment and falling incomes. Therefore, the service industries which catered to the resident population faced a contracting market. The government suffered a declining tax base. For the younger and better trained workers, few opportunities were available. So they left, in large numbers, robbing the area of some of its most skilled, vigorous and productive workers.

The decline in economic activity, employment, investment and consumer expenditure lowered the income of the region. Land values fell and the tax base weakened. Local governments faced one of two alternatives, both undesirable. Either they could reduce expenditures on education, transportation facilities and on social and economic support services (what economists call "infrastructure"); or they could maintain expenditures and increase taxes. Either alternative could only serve to further depress investment and employment opportunities and with them, regional income — this is the meaning of the circle of underdevelopment. Low incomes mean low expenditures; low expenditures mean low investment opportunities; low investment opportunities mean low employment opportunities and low productivity; low employment and productivity mean low incomes and savings. What is true for the underdeveloped countries of Africa, Asia or South America is also true for the Atlantic, northern or western hinterlands of Canada.

The Resource Hinterland

The postwar trend in the Canadian economy has been increasing dependence on foreign demand for resources and foreign capital for the development of these resources. Historically, natural resources in Canada have been exploited primarily for the benefit of other countries. For example, pulp and paper and minerals were dependent on the industrial needs of the American industrial system. INCO was incorporated as a Canadian company early in this century but it remains an American-controlled company, despite a high level of Canadian share ownership. It incorporated in Canada to escape American anti-trust laws that would have forced it to break up its monopoly control of the nickel industry. The U.S. Commission on Materials Policy indicates that foreign resources have become increasingly important to the country's manufacturing industry and Canada is one of its prime sources.

Table 5-1

U.S. IMPORTS OF RESOURCES

Material	Imports as a Per cent of U.S. Consumption		
	1950	*1970*	*1985 forecast*
Zinc	37	60	73
Manganese	77	94	100
Titanium	32	47	n.a.
Aluminum	71	86	98
Petroleum	8	22	n.a.
Iron Ore	6	14	55
Platinum	91	98	n.a.
Cobalt	92	96	n.a.
Natural Gas	0	3	n.a.
Chromium	100	100	100
Tin	100	100	100
Timber	11	8	n.a.
Nickel	99	91	88
Lead	59	40	61
Copper	35	8	34
Tungsten	80	40	87
Mercury	92	38	n.a.

By 1970, 76 per cent of Canada's oil and gas industry and 70 per cent of the mining industry was foreign controlled. Foreign control comprised around 96 per cent of petroleum processing and 48 per cent of pulp and paper manufacturing. During their development phases those industries brought construction jobs sinking the shafts and drill holes, building the mills and refineries. Some permanent jobs were available in the pulp mills, the mines and smelters, but they were relatively few. In 1971, the mining industry provided jobs for only 1.6 per cent of the Canadian labour force, the same percentage as in 1921 and down from 2.2 per cent in 1941. Forestry was even smaller, employing less than one per cent of the labour force in 1971, down from 2.2 per cent in 1941 and 1.3 per cent in 1921. Forestry actually provided 20,000 fewer jobs in 1971 than 30 years earlier. Meanwhile, employment in pulp and paper, the big growth industry, was less than one per cent of the labour force in 1971. In total, forestry and pulp and paper, mining, smelting and refining employed less than 4 per cent of the Canadian labour force in 1971 — fewer than the number of people employed in hospitals in the country. Resource industries have brought little permanent development but have left a heritage of a dual economy that has increased the inequality between and within regions.

The Manufacturing Sector

The postwar boom in foreign investment in resource exploitation is one manifestation of the disintegration of the national economy in Canada in favour of a series of regional economies whose destinies are inextricably bound to economic decisions made outside the country. The manufacturing sector has not escaped either. In fact, as foreign control has increased, its role in the Canadian economy has weakened. In 1954, 51 per cent of Canadian manufacturing was controlled by foreigners. By 1970 this had risen to 61 per cent. Manufacturing employment in Canada in 1946 accounted for 25 per cent of the labour force; by 1973, this had fallen to 22 per cent. Obviously, the growth in these goods-producing sectors was insufficient to absorb the growing labour force and the steady influx of rural migrants displaced from the land by the rapid growth in farm size and the growing reliance on the import of foreign foods.

The problem has been particularly acute in provinces which have a large agriculture and primary industry population and a proportionately small manufacturing sector. What manufacturing there is tends to be concentrated in processing raw materials or in serving the rural and service population with the kind of goods that are produced in small plants. This includes goods that are perishable, cannot stand long transportation or are tailored to the localized market — for example, bakeries, milk processing, printing, sash and door mills, butter and cheese plants and numerous other miscellaneous small manufactures. These are important and necessary industries, but not the base of a diversified, developed economy. Their capacity to absorb labour is limited, particularly as their regional market shrinks. They offer few opportunities for the young and better educated workers who are therefore forced to seek opportunities outside the region. The decreasing population has a growing average age and therefore a rising dependent group that adds to the economic burden of those who remain, by choice or lack of alternatives.

Continental Integration

Dominance by the continental American economy and the multinational corporation has effectively made the regions of Canada into regions of the American economy. The very thing that the national policy and Confederation were designed to prevent has come about, partly because of the national policy itself and very much because the national policy, as it became progressively outmoded, was not adapted to changing economic needs. Indeed, the Canadian government appears to have abandoned any pretence of a national policy.

This has a number of serious implications for Canada. Perhaps the single most obvious one is that the economy, structured this way, cannot be controlled by economic policies implemented by the federal government. Continental integration in the postwar period has placed the overall level of economic activity in Canada beyond Ottawa's control. This means that federal economic policies have become incapable of offsetting the cyclical instabilities of the economy or of affecting the regional inequalities and structural problems that have beset the country. Government has surrendered control over investment to the multinational corporations, yet the amount and distribution of investment is in fact the prime determinant of both the growth and distribution of economic activity in the country.

After the great depression of the 1930s, the Canadian government adopted the policy recommendations of the English economist, John Maynard Keynes. In simple terms, Keynes argued that when an economy was depressed, the government should use fiscal policy (expanding government expenditure, reducing taxation and increasing income transfers to people) and monetary policy (reducing interest rates and increasing the supply of money) to stimulate the economy. By lowering taxes, increasing government expenditures and income transfers, more expenditure would take place, increasing employment and encouraging businesses to expand. By lowering interest rates and making credit more available, the cost of borrowing money would be reduced and businesses would find it more profitable to invest, adding further to the stimulus of the economy. Keynes's policy recommendations made a great deal of sense, in theory. But the rise to economic dominance of the multinational corporations which operate in more than one country and which, therefore, can stand aloof from the economic policy of most individual nations has fundamentally altered the effectiveness of Keynes's recommended measures to influence the overall level of economic activity.

This is particularly true of Canada, which is not only small in relation to these corporations, but is so integrated with the American economy that the policies of that country are far more powerful in affecting investment in Canada than is Canadian policy. This is a direct consequence of the continental integration of the investment markets.

A few examples will illustrate the difficulties this country now confronts. In the face of the current depression, the Bank of Canada (at least in theory), could try to lower interest rates to encourage investors to spend more on new capital expenditures. But there is no guarantee that the multinational companies, even if they do take advantage of the cheaper money, will increase total investment in Canada. They may in fact borrow in Canada and invest in Guatemala, Brazil, South Africa or Indonesia. (They might not do so directly. What they can do is take the profits earned in Canada and send them to some other country and use the borrowed money to replace this export of capital.) Further, this demand for investment money which would be used elsewhere in the world would have the effect of driving the interest rate in Canada back up, at least to the American rate, preventing smaller firms not operating on a multinational scale from benefiting from the policy. One rather dubious advantage that could result would be a fall in the value of the Canadian dollar that should increase world demand for Canadian exports and lower Canadian demand for imports. But it would also have the effect of increasing the prices of all imported goods, which would mean inflationary pressures for consumers and producers in Canada. In fact in 1978, the Bank of Canada has been following the opposite policy, driving up interest rates, in order to protect the already weakened value of the Canadian dollar.

Of course, following Keynes's recipe may lead to some increased investment in Canada. But if the economy is already depressed, why would firms want to increase investment? In the hinterland regions, investment in resource development will occur only when the American market expands so that the demand for Canadian resources improves. If investment occurs in manufacturing, it will occur in the already concentrated heartland around the Great Lakes. This might improve employment in that area, if markets can be found for the goods produced. But the multinational companies buy a disproportionate share of their inputs, particularly of machinery and equipment, through their parent operations in the United States. So if there is any expansionary effect of the policy, much of it will leak out of the country into the United States. And if this investment occurs without any overall improvement in the Canadian economy, it will almost inevitably be in new plant and equipment that will be labour saving. The final result can easily be fewer jobs, not more jobs, in the Canadian economy.

If monetary policy (such as reducing interest rates) in these circumstances is, at best, ineffective, what about fiscal policy like increased government spending or reduced taxes? Federal, provincial and local governments have increased their expenditures markedly in recent years although the rise in government purchases of goods and services has been small compared with the rise in transfer payments — unemployment insurance and welfare payments, family and mothers' allowances, pensions and similar transfers. In part, this has been because of the depressed economy and regional offsets to disparities. Without this increased spending, the economy would have been in even worse shape than it is, and many Canadians would have been much worse off, but the problems remain.

What about decreasing taxes? The first question about this approach is, whose taxes? A general cut in income taxes would be politically popular but it is unlikely to do much to help the depressed regions. If it causes Canadians to increase their spending, most of it will flow either to the central manufacturing area or to the American, Japanese or other economies which now supply Canada with so much of its food and manufactured goods. The resource industries would see few benefits. And even a small income tax cut would severely undermine the government budgets that are already stretched to the limit. This would necessitate a cutback in government programs and transfers to the poorer people and the poorer regions. And a tax cut limited to the poor, who now pay relatively little in taxes, would have little impact. The net result is likely to be an increase in inequality and unemployment.

Business would of course rather see cuts in business taxes — despite the fact that, as Eric Kierans has pointed out, Canada already has one of the most generous packages in the western world of tax benefits, subsidies, write-offs, subsidized loans, depletion and depreciation allowances, tax deferrals, capital grants and other corporate welfare provisions. Corporate profits in the five-year period from 1970 to 1975 increased 131 per cent, from $7.7 billion to $17.8 billion. Corporate wealth increased from $190 billion in 1968 to $427 billion in 1974, a 17 per cent compound growth rate. Now the request is for more tax relief to encourage investment. But will the multinational corporations use the decreased taxes to increase investment?

In the case of the oil companies, spokesmen argued that domestic prices would have to rise to provide increased profits to pay for increased exploration. The Canadian and Alberta governments complied and while oil profits rose 23 per cent between 1974 and 1975, Canadian exploration expenditures declined by 3 per cent.

Even if investment expenditures are increased, there is reason to doubt that this expenditure will take place in Canada. The Canadian mineral industry evidence is not reassuring. Profits in the nickel industry in Canada have been used to develop mines in Guatemala and Indonesia and to experiment with the recovery of undersea nickel-bearing nodules. But in 1977-78 massive layoffs were announced in Sudbury and Thompson. In Newfoundland, the fluorspar mine of Alcan was shut down in 1977, even though it was profitable, because the multinational could buy its inputs cheaper outside the country. In any case, investment in resource-based industry really depends on the demand for those resources, again primarily from the United States. While demand is depressed, Canadian policy can have little expansionary effect. And even if demand does pick up there is no assurance that tax concessions will result in increased investment in Canada if the funds can find more lucrative opportunities elsewhere.

Much the same situation applies in the tariff-supported manufacturing industries. Reducing their taxes would add to their profits. But a manufacturing firm would not use those increased profits to expand capacity when, as has been the case since 1976, there is already 20 per cent or more idle plant in Canadian industry, due to lack of markets. What is more likely is that these profits would be repatriated to the foreign head office to be used in another country or distributed to foreign stockholders. Or these profits would be used by the corporations to buy up their own stock, thereby increasing the concentration of wealth in fewer and fewer hands; or to buy up smaller firms through takeovers and mergers, again concentrating wealth and market power in the hands of a smaller number of larger corporations. And these larger corporations produce more output with fewer workers, in effect replacing labour with capitalized profits.

Unreal Expectations

Many economists argue that replacement investment in existing industries, when it takes place, will occur in the depressed regions of the country, to take advantage of lower wages and surplus labour. The fact that this has rarely occurred anywhere in the western world in the postwar period has not shaken the faith of the Economic Council of Canada in this proposition. Even if it does happen, a multinational corporation is unlikely to relocate a labour-intensive plant in the Maritimes, where average wages are only 15 per cent lower than in Ontario, or in Quebec where they average 5 per cent lower, or in Manitoba where they are 10 per cent lower. They locate in the Phillipines, Korea, Taiwan, Hong Kong or Brazil, where wages are 80 or 90 per cent lower and where oppressive governments prevent the organization of labour unions that would protect the workers from exploitation.

The Location of Subsidiaries

The location of subsidiary operations of American multinationals in Canada is, in fact, determined not primarily by Canadian economics, but by where the head offices in the United States are located. A Canadian geographer, Michael Ray, has made a series of studies of the location of U.S. multinationals in Canada and comes to the conclusion that branch plants are located in Canada so as to be as close as possible to the parent head office. For example, Winnipeg is more likely to get a branch plant if the head office is in Minneapolis than if it is in Boston or New York, while Vancouver is more likely to get a branch plant if the head office is in California rather than in Chicago or Detroit. But at the same time, he also notes that income disparities in Canada are much greater between regions than they are between cities in those same regions, i.e. the overall disparities between Ontario and the Atlantic region are much greater than the disparities between Hamilton or Toronto and Halifax or Saint John. He concludes, therefore, that any attack on regional disparities in Canada must involve more balanced urban growth rates between different regions in the country. This implies furthermore that, since one of the most important elements in generating urban growth is the expansion in manufacturing, the location of multinationals, with their control over more than half of all Canadian manufacturing, is crucial in deciding where urban growth occurs in Canada.

In 1961, of 1,618 U.S. subsidiaries in Canada 1,132 or 70 per cent were located in the southwestern section of

Ontario that includes Toronto. Comparable data on non-U.S. controlled multinationals are not available; while they are probably not as regionally concentrated as U.S. subsidiaries, there is still a tendency for large scale multinationals to cluster together.

Table 5-2

PERCENTAGE OF REGIONAL MANUFACTURING CONTROLLED BY U.S. SUBSIDIARIES IN 1970

Region	Measured by Employment	Measured by Manuf. Net Output
Atlantic	12.5	15.6
Quebec	27.8	34.5
Ontario	46.0	52.1
Prairies	22.0	27.7
B.C. (incl. Yukon and N.W.T.)	27.9	30.3

Why is foreign manufacturing investment so much more concentrated in Central Canada than Canadian manufacturing investment? There are two reasons. Multinational companies are overrepresented by the large, oligopolistic, mass production industries which serve a wide, national market and which congregate in industrial areas; whereas Canadian firms are on average smaller, involved in light consumer industries serving local markets, and therefore more likely to reflect the distribution of the population. Michael Ray's research offers a second important reason: Canadian subsidiaries of U.S. corporations locate as close to their American parent as the borders and potential market permit. Thus Canadian industry is concentrated in southern Ontario, where it is closest geographically to the head offices of multinational corporations in the United States.

The Failure of Policy Response

The main attempt by the Canadian government to counteract the forces fragmenting the Canadian economy, as we have already shown, has been the Department of Regional Economic Expansion. Most of DREE's efforts have been in the field of upgrading community services and facilities to improve the attractiveness of depressed regions to investors. But it is its program of incentive grants, to induce firms to locate or relocate in less favoured areas, that has drawn most criticism. There are good grounds for criticism of both the rationale of DREE incentive grants and the actual success of the grant program.

From the inception of the grant program in 1969 until 1976, DREE claims to have assisted in the creation of some 124,828 jobs, 88 per cent in the "have not" provinces. Even if we accept DREE's own estimate, labour force growth over the same period in Canada was around two million. At best, therefore, DREE grants of over half a billion dollars have assisted in the creation of jobs for about 6 per cent of the growth in the labour force (ignoring those workers who became unemployed through technological changes). The direct cost of each assisted job was more than $4,400, excluding all other expenditures by DREE to improve the economic climate in those regions receiving assistance. (Incentive grants represented only 18 per cent of DREE expenditures in 1975-76.) If, as Halifax economist Mike Bradfield has suggested, 35 per cent of other DREE expenditures are necessary to provide the basic economic infrastructure to support those grants, the cost of each job in direct and indirect subsidies works out to be approximately $10,000.

In spite of this level of expenditure, there are few indications that there has been a significant reduction in regional disparities, or more significantly, in the critical area of the distribution of manufacturing. Nor is this surprising. Studies by David Springate and Carlton Dudley on the effects of location grants explore the reasons for the ineffectiveness of incentive grants in promoting the kind of secondary manufacturing industries that increase industrial development. Springate bases his work on investigations of investment decisions by large companies, the kind of major projects that have been the target for regional programs. His findings are that grants are not of much use in attracting investment for a number of reasons:

- Decision-makers operate from personal knowledge and therefore "consider geographical areas which they know or feel to be conducive to successful operations". This usually means choosing locations close to existing plants.
- The location decision is usually a technical decision, made by technical staff who do not consider grants.
- In picking the region for location, the prime considerations are those of operating and transportation costs, labour force availability and costs, marketing considerations and, infrequently, political considerations. Grants are only influential in locating investment within regions.
- Firms avoid the risk which is associated with less industrially developed regions.
- Businessmen prefer not to be influenced by government grant programs.

He also notes that many companies do not contact DREE until after the location decision has been made, which suggests that the grants constitute more of a windfall profit to large corporations than a significant influence on the location of their investment.

In a more theoretical vein, Dudley offers strong support for Springate's findings. Grants, he finds, have at best only a very small effect on operating cost, and secondly:

The possibility of significant incentive assistance tends to be biased in favour of the more capital intensive industries, which tend to have few, large installations. Thus the program has by nature rather little to offer to many of the secondary manufacturing industries, those that are particularly desired for their development potential.

It is possible that capital grants may encourage plants to adopt more capital intensive methods than they would otherwise, thereby actually reducing the number of new jobs made available. In fact, if a company is big, it may drive out of existence smaller, more labour intensive businesses already established in the region.

It is also quite possible that the only plants whose locations can be influenced by grants are those that are marginal operations. Inducing them to locate in depressed areas merely perpetuates a marginal economy. This is supported by studies in the Maritimes which found that employment instability was greater in cases of subsidized operations. Probably the best known cases include Clairtone and the Japanese CMI auto plant, both of which were induced into the region by subsidies and which have since ceased production. Furthermore, 85 per cent of the firms which received Canadian grants were foreign owned and, therefore, dependent on decisions made in other countries and not responsive to Canadian needs and policies.

It is, of course, unfair to blame continuing inequality solely on the one federal agency charged with combating regional disparities. The fundamental problem lies with those elements of the contemporary structure and behaviour of the Canadian market economy that perpetuate disparities in spite of attempts, no matter how small or poorly conceived, to correct them. The most important question is why the big, stable corporations don't move into the hinterland regions. The answer is that they do — when it is in their economic interest to do so. But there is no guarantee that if they do, that development will result. Resource-based companies, of course, must locate at the source of the resource. As often as not, the location of these is in remote places, away from the available labour force. As a result, governments must usually provide roads, schools and social facilities. In exchange, the government benefits from the jobs, and the tax and royalty revenues. But if the tax and royalty revenues have been given away to attract the "development", only the jobs, usually few in number with resource projects, are left to justify the generally large public investment.

If a province attempts to raise its resource income, the multinationals often have the option of going elsewhere where more pliant governments are less demanding. (The cost of the mining concession for the INCO mine in Guatemala was obtained for $20,000 a year.) Unless the public is willing to nationalize and operate the plant, it is caught between the low revenues which alternative underdeveloped areas are willing to accept, and plant closure — or no plant at all.

What about the income and jobs these resources generate in Canada in processing and manufacturing? Because these industries feed the import needs of other regions and countries, particularly the United States, very little processing is done at the Canadian source other than the first stages such as concentrating, smelting, some refining in mining, pulping and newsprint-making in pulp and paper. These are extremely capital intensive processes requiring relatively small labour forces. The higher-order, secondary manufacturing industries are located in southern Ontario or the United States or Japan. One major grievance of Quebec regarding the American-owned asbestos industry is that only a tiny fraction (around 3 per cent), of the asbestos mined in the province is processed in Quebec (or even in Canada), the primary source of asbestos for the western world. Only provincial ownership or tough government regulations can do much to change the situation.

All these resource regions are vulnerable to fluctuations in foreign demand and to changes in foreign import policy (such as the tariffs or quotas demanded in the winter of 1977-78 by U.S. producers of zinc and copper to protect their interests in times of slack demand), and to the discovery of alternative sources of supply. They are also sensitive to fluctuations in exchange rates. In

short, these regions are not masters of their own houses
— this is the meaning of dependency.

Secondary manufacturers, particularly multinationals,
do not locate in depressed regions, despite the attraction
of lower wages. Manufacturers of consumer goods like
to be near their markets. Where are their markets?
Where the people are. Where are the people? Where the
jobs are. Where are the jobs? Where manufacturing is
concentrated. Once the process of concentration begins,
it is hard to reverse. Manufacturers of parts, machinery
and equipment also like to be near their markets. Where
are these markets? Where the manufacturers of consumer goods are. Head office businessmen and financial
officers like to be in close contact with one another.
Where are other businessmen and financial officers?
Where firms are concentrated. Where are firms concentrated? Where manufacturers, banks and financial institutions are concentrated.

The iron law of industrial concentration is that industry attracts industry, that firms locate and expand as close
as they can to their existing localities and to other industry unless there is a compelling reason for them to
relocate. Even Montreal, the oldest business centre in
Canada, with its historic basis in Canadian trade with
Europe, cannot withstand the attraction of Toronto and
southern Ontario, with its historic basis in the American
economic connection. The stronger that economic connection, the weaker became the economic basis of
Montreal and the industrial area of Quebec. Unless new
federal economic policies are forthcoming to stop the de-
development of Quebec, the province has only one alternative to prevent its continuing slide into further
dependency — separation.

Unfortunately, federal policy, far from combating the
concentration of secondary manufacturing, has aided it,
most noticeably and persistently through the discrimina-
tory freight rate structure, but also in numerous other
ways.

The Technology Gap

Canada's poor performance in combating regional disparities owes something to its record in the area of research and development (R & D), particularly in developing production technology suitable to the small and fragmented Canadian economy. Overall Canadian R & D spending is very low. The recent report of the Special Committee of the Senate on Science Policy placed Canada amongst the lowest of western industrialized countries as measured by the proportion of national income invested in R & D. The low level is compounded by the fact that the proportion has been falling fairly steadily in recent years, from 1.24 per cent in 1970 to 1.03 per cent in 1976, according to the Senate report. Much of this effort in private sector R & D is restricted to downsizing or adapting American technology for the smaller Canadian economy. Industry funds less than one third of Canadian R & D; governments fund the biggest proportion, 50 per cent.

Dependency on foreign, mainly American, technology contributes to the regionalized structure of the Canadian economy. Use of this mass scale technology in Canada, even in scaled-down form, commits production to take place in one centralized location where economies of scale can be maximized. Given the existing distribution of population and industry and the structure of freight rates, this means continued concentration in southern Ontario. Reinforcing this tendency is the major role played by the multinationals in R & D. They are centralized in southern Ontario, and the result is that so is this activity. Technical and scientific graduates in the hinterland regions of Canada find that what jobs exist in their fields are concentrated in the industrial heartland. In the manufacturing sector, the leading industries in terms of employers of scientists and engineers are the electrical, chemical, transportation equipment, metals and paper industries. These are the very industries that comprise a disproportionate share of Ontario's manufacturing base relative to the rest of Canada.

Foreign control of manufacturing and resource production stands in the way of the development of policy to reverse these tendencies in the field of R & D and industrial technology. A study by H. Crookell of the impact of integration of Canadian and American manufacturing has noted that closer ties between industries in the two countries (along the lines of the Auto Pact) removes the capacity in Canada not just for innovation but also for management of industry:

> If the other rationalized industries behave like the auto makers and rationalize operations from a production standpoint only, then another Canadian industry would lose its managerial and professional staff and with them any hope of innovating in the future. *To lose its power to innovate in a changing environment is to yield control of the future to those who retain that power.*

So while the multinational control of manufacturing contributes directly to regional imbalances in economic activity and opportunity, it has a more serious long-term impact in that by removing the ability to innovate, it destroys the opportunity to develop an effective national policy to counteract regional disparities.

The automobile industry's history, particularly since the 1965 Auto Pact, illustrates this process. The Science Council in 1971 noted the lack of "the kind of indirect benefit that should flow from the production and marketing of products as sophisticated as a motor vehicle, particularly where the market is of a size that could support more balanced development and production processes". Instead, Canada's role in auto production has been progressively more concentrated in the least sophisticated areas of the industry. A recent study of the Department of Industry, Trade and Commerce documents some of these results. The Canadian trade deficit in automobiles reached $2 billion in 1975. While Canada's share of total employment has risen, the gain has been at the lower end of the skill and income scale. In the United States, 49 per cent of automobile workers are unskilled; 43 per cent are semi-skilled and 8 per cent are skilled. In Canada, 75 per cent are unskilled, 23 per cent are semi-skilled and 2 per cent are skilled. The inferior position of Canada is also reflected on the investment side. Over the 1973-75 period, investment by the automobile industry in Canada was a mere 5 per cent of the total.

In contrast to the results in the automobile industry, the example of Northern Electric (now Northern Telecom) gives some indication of the potential for a national policy. In 1956, Northern Electric, a Canadian subsidiary of the American-based Western Electric, and dependent on Western Electric for its technology, was cut loose from its American parent as a result of American anti-trust law. Forced to rely on its own resources (particularly technological), Northern, rather than suffering a setback, began to develop indigenous Canadian capability:

Table 5-3

SELECTED DEVELOPMENT INDICATORS: NORTHERN ELECTRIC

	1958	1969
Professional staff	3(1957)	727
R & D Employees	55	2,037
R & D Division Expenditures ($000)	329.6	30,503.0
Suppliers:		
Raw materials and basic supplies		
Canada	88%	93%
U.S.	12%	7%
Components		
Canada	62%	85%
U.S.	38%	15%

In addition, exports as a percentage of total sales have risen from 2.5 per cent in 1963 to 24.8 per cent in 1974 as Northern developed reliance on its own technological capabilities.

Unless Canada can reassert control of its own economy and arrest its slide into dependency on the American economy, it will continue to lose control of its own economic policy. Without this power any attempt to reduce economic disparities between regions will be largely ineffectual. One should expect that Ottawa would be directing its attention to a new industrial strategy that would unite the country in a national economic unit within which regional policy could be integrated. Unfortunately, it appears that the opposite is happening. Recent press reports from Ottawa and comments by the Minister of Finance, supported by the American ambassador and leaders of multinational business, advocate more integration with U.S. industry — that is, more auto pacts. The prospects are not reassuring.

Summary

The only conclusion that can be drawn from recent economic experience is that the federal government has virtually lost control of national economic policy. It has, in practice, accepted that the nation should be a series of dependent regions of the U.S. economy. While Liberal governments have been the most active proponents of continental integration, Conservative policies have dissented not on principle, but only on the terms of surrender. Some provincial governments, lacking the levers of power, have tried, with little success, to reverse the erosion of domestic decision-making.

The resource industries in hinterland regions that serve export markets are dependent on foreign economic conditions for their level of employment and rate of growth. When demand is high, waves of investment flood in, straining the capacity of local services and the construction industry. When demand falls, widespread unemployment and depressed local incomes result. Except in the construction stages, these industries seldom purchase their inputs from the local or regional economy. The regional development that results is minimal, providing unstable though often well-paying jobs for the frequently small number of workers who remain to operate the mines and mills.

Canada's manufacturing industries tend to concentrate in southern Ontario; in the case of U.S. subsidiaries, this means staying close to their parents and to the largest part of the Canadian market. The U.S. subsidiaries are relatively unresponsive to Canadian government policy since their market is more or less restricted to domestic demand. But domestic demand is relatively little influenced by monetary and fiscal policy because of the continental integration of the economy. The major multinational resource and manufacturing corporations are able to circumvent Canadian policy. The world is their playground and the policies recommended in the 1930s by Keynes to control overall economic growth and investment hardly touch them.

As long as Canada is merely a branch-plant, down-sized economy using borrowed technology, it can never expect to develop the kind of technical advantage in new products, new processes and new designs that are the secret to amplifying markets beyond the domestic borders. As long as decision-making power, the ability to innovate and the independence to seek export markets is beyond the country's grasp, regional policy must merely be a defensive stance. The answer to Canada's economic disintegration must lie in an aggressive economic policy to reassert control of the economy's direction. Dependency on foreign demand and foreign capital is a risky, and as we are learning, ultimately a fatal game. Without a national strategy of economic development, the hinterland regions must continue to operate in a policy vacuum and have little hope for any substantially different position inside the Canadian economy.

6
Rebuilding the Economy: A New National Policy

While the very political existence of the Canadian nation is being questioned, federalists, led by Ottawa politicians who are unusually unanimous on the point, have turned an uncompromising face to Quebec. Few proposals have surfaced outside of that province to revamp the existing structure of Confederation in a way that would accommodate Quebec's aspirations. Nor has the federal government made any substantial efforts to get at the economic roots of provincial disaffection.

It is, of course, true that Quebec's quest for sovereignty is not totally economic in motivation, but has a strong cultural and linguistic component. But, as we have already argued, these are not unconnected. As long as the business of Quebec is conducted in English, the avenues to economic power are blocked to Francophones and while Bill 101, particularly the head office guidelines on the language of business, is intended to change this situation, it may merely result in the relocation of the top managerial and technical functions outside the province. Furthermore, the dominance of the multinational corporations results in what in the underdeveloped economies is called "cocacolonization", the overwhelming of an indigenous culture with an imported one. In its urgency for economic independence from Anglo-Canadian control, the P.Q. has not faced up to the reality that American control is, in the long run, a much more pervasive threat to Quebec's unique culture.

In order to have a society strong enough to foster and protect its culture, Quebec needs a well-developed economy which will provide the options and the resources necessary to exercise these options. As industry, particularly that which is expanding and technologically advanced, continues to shift west into southern Ontario, the economic base of Quebec society "de-develops". If plans (presently being discussed in Ottawa) to reduce tariff barriers with the United States and to create a number of new auto-pact type integrations of North American industry, with Canada concentrating on a few, world-scale, high-technology export industries go through, the present base of the Quebec economy will be destroyed. Such a federal scenario virtually forces the withdrawal of the province from Confederation so that it can protect the economic base needed to ensure its continued cultural existence.

While this argument has been put in terms of Quebec's situation, much the same is true, to a greater or lesser extent, of other hinterland regions of Canada. The uneven and unequal distribution of economic activity and opportunity in Canada has created tremendous tensions and consequent political instabilities.

Policies of the past are no answer to the current crisis. After all, the branch plant and regional nature of the current Canadian economy is, in large measure, the result of Macdonald's 1879 National Policy of protection. It is also doubtful whether or not the rest of the country will want to pay the price for protecting Quebec's labour-intensive clothing, shoe and textile industries from import competition. Nor would increased protection do much to diversify industry out of southern Ontario and into the depressed regions or do anything to decrease the branch plant mentality or to increase research and development.

It bears repeating that in a depressed economy with

stagnant or declining investment, the opportunity for regional diversification of industry is not only limited, it is precluded. *No regional development policy is possible without a national development strategy* that opens up opportunities for and sources of expanded investment in the hinterland areas. This requires a new set of policies, or a new national policy, backed by a national commitment to the task of reducing regional disparities — of reducing the dependent nature of the Canadian economy and the regional inequality inherent in that dependency.

No national strategy will have much prospect of acceptance if it merely tries to reallocate existing economic activity. The key, therefore, is to find new opportunities, new sources of capital and new entrepreneurial vehicles with which to tackle the problem. To do that, the country's strength in natural resources must be integrated with Canadian entrepreneurship and technologies appropriate to the size and geography of the Canadian market.

What would such a strategy look like? It would look very similar to Canada's economic policy during the Second World War, which was designed to create as rapidly as possible the industrial capacity needed to support its war effort. Again the government must take the lead, but the battle it must fight this time is not the enemy outside but the disintegration within. The tools that it has are the nation's resource riches to provide the capital, and the existing, underutilized investment in education and training of the Canadian labour force to provide the expertise. The three components of such a strategy, therefore, are natural resource policy, research and development policy and public entrepreneurship.

Natural Resources

Resource rich nations that continually yield up the value of their wealth in return for the labour employed in its exploitation will never be more than resource nations. They lose the opportunity to form their own capital, capital which will enable them to break out of that very reliance on their resource base and reduce their dependence on foreign investment. When a nation or province can generate capital out of its own resources and retain it, it will be less dependent on others.

The critical element in economic development everywhere is the allocation of the economic surplus, that value of output over and above what is necessary to maintain the existing level of production. For practical purposes in the contemporary economy, the economic surplus includes savings, profits, interest on investments and economic rent (the value of natural resources over and above what it costs to extract them, including normal profits). This is the total value that can be used to increase the wealth of the nation in the form of productive investment.

What is vitally important, of course, is what that surplus is used for and where the surplus is used. Unless some mechanisms are employed to ensure that the surplus is invested in the poorer regions, these regions must forever remain disadvantaged relative to the richer regions. Policies to ensure the retention of investment for the processing of natural resources are not new in Canada by any means. The Ontario and Quebec governments around the turn of the century fostered the development of the pulp and paper industry by restricting the export of unprocessed wood pulp to the United States and, more recently in the 1950s and 1960s, the British Columbia government encouraged the establishment of pulp and paper mills in the province by restricting terms of forest licences. But except in the field of energy, little systematic use has been made of restrictive export policies as a mechanism for economic development based on natural resources.

The one major source of surplus available to Canadian policy-makers is the economic rent from natural resources, whether it is appropriated by taxes, royalties or public ownership. Both Alberta and Saskatchewan have begun to realize the potential of natural resources as a heritage for the future despite federal government tactics to limit the ability of the provinces to collect the resource revenues. Ottawa disallowed provincial royalties as a deductible expense for purposes of assessing federal income taxes, a move which obstructed the tendency of some provinces to increase taxes that would appropriate a greater share of economic rents for the public. Ottawa, in contrast to the two western provinces, does not have any development strategy to utilize resource income for investment purposes.

There is, of course, a degree of urgency in the case of non-renewable resources. The longer governments delay, the more high grade resources will be utilized, which means the lower the economic rent. This can be illustrated simply. If the price of a mineral is $1.00 a pound and the costs of production of high grade reserves, including "normal profits" is $.90 a pound, the economic rent is $.10. If this rent is not captured and the prime reserves give out so that the costs of production rise to $.98 a pound, the economic rent falls to $.02. Obviously, this is an oversimplification, because the world price of resources rises and falls depending on the state of the international economy. But it is close enough to suggest a degree of urgency in public policy — before the best resources become exhausted. And the cheaper we let our resources go for, the faster they will disappear. As Eric Kierans has documented, the public has not been capturing much of the economic rent. In the 1959-65 period, for example, public revenues from the exploitation of metallic mineral resources in Manitoba averaged less than 15 per cent of profits, with private returns capturing more than 85 per cent.

This does not mean that it is easy for governments to appropriate the rents. One alternative is to set taxes or royalties at such a level that the rent accrues to the federal or provincial governments. But the taxation of resource companies is fraught with difficulties. If Canadian governments attempt to collect rents through income taxes or royalties while governments in other resource-producing countries or regions do not, the large corporations will merely shift their production to the low tax jurisdictions. Alternatively, these companies can shift their profits to low tax jurisdictions — such as the tax havens of Lichtenstein, Switzerland, Panama, the Bahamas or the Netherland Antilles — by manipulating transfer prices (that is, the prices that one branch of a corporation in one country or region charges its other branches in other areas for goods and services transferred between the two branches). Short of an international, government-organized cartel on the OPEC model, therefore, the opportunity for capturing natural resource rents for development purposes through taxation and royalties is limited.

On the other hand, if the rents aren't captured they may be lost to Canadian development. If the rents remain in the hands of the large multinationals, the developmental impact will be left to the chance discovery of more resources and to world demand. There is virtually no mechanism that will transfer multinational profits into regional diversification or measures of regional equalization.

It was such difficulties, compounded by federal tax policies, that induced the Saskatchewan government to nationalize a large part of its potash industry. Although it has not been necessary to do this in oil because of the OPEC pricing policies and the huge size of the rents and profits in the industry, public ownership is one of the most efficient ways of accumulating this surplus from resources for the development of regional industry. But whatever the method, Alberta's and Saskatchewan's heritage funds indicate what can be done to create a base for regional development.

The Technological Imperative

Even if investment capital is available in Canada under Canadian control there is no guarantee that it will be utilized in a way that will attack regional disparities in the economy. One major problem is that the technology most readily available in Canada is American; it is large scale, mass production technology that does not fit well the Canadian market, which is one-tenth the size of the American and more dispersed and fragmented. What is required is the development of our own technology, one which recognizes the limitations of the Canadian market and is not dependent on centralized, large scale production.

Native innovative capacity is crucial to regional development for another important reason. Any industrial society that does not innovate, that does not adjust technology to its changing economic needs and to the needs of export markets is bound to stagnate. This not only limits the opportunities for new investment, it contributes to slow employment, income and productivity growth, which serve to feed both unemployment and inflation.

It is imperative that a national program of research and development be undertaken, because without it, no coherent national strategy can be realized. And without a national strategy, hopes for regional policies are dim. If the private sector is unwilling or unable to take the lead because it is foreign owned or because Canadian firms are too small or too conservative, then it is up to government and the universities to take the initiative.

The Public as Entrepreneur

Even with available capital and appropriate technology someone has to take on the role of entrepreneur, the agency that puts the elements together into an economic package. As Herschel Hardin wrote in *A Nation Unaware*:

> Canada, in its essentials, is a public enterprise country, always has been, and probably always will be. Americans have, or at least had, a genius for private enterprise; Canadians have a genius for public enterprise.... Once the powerful impulse of Canadian na-

tionalism combines with a liberated public enterprise culture, Canada will experience a golden age of entrepreneurship, because nothing in modern times is quite so creative as practical self-discovery.

Unfortunately, Hardin argues, Canadians have succumbed to what he calls "the American ideology in Canada", and despite the historical fact that the main source of vigorous entrepreneurship for the big, tough problems of economic development has been the public sector and not the private, Canadians overlook this heritage when considering solutions to current economic problems.

Part of the explanation of this public entrepreneurship culture lies in the smallness of the Canadian economy alongside that of its giant neighbour. Few Canadian firms have the resources to enter into or withstand protracted competition with much larger American firms, particularly in heavily capitalized industries or in those dependent on the expensive and risky business of technological innovation. Yet when Canadians have understood the problem to be a major one, governments have successfully met the challenge — creating a national radio and TV network and an airline, massive provincially-owned hydro systems and high technology breakthroughs in synthetic rubber, atomic energy and short takeoff and landing aircraft, to name some of the examples.

The example of Canada's wartime economic policy in the area of industrial development is instructive. Under the tutelage of C.D. Howe (no left-winger by any means), the government in its haste to meet the industrial needs of war, used the Department of Munitions and Supply to create 28 crown corporations, several in high technology industries (including Polymer), but many others in the secondary manufacturing sector. When industrial development became critical to Canada's existence, even businessmen turned to the agency of public entrepreneurship for the answer. In the current economic crisis of national disintegration, perhaps the only viable strategy is a repeat performance — with regional disparities the avowed enemy.

A National Strategy

Thus, we can identify the three elements of a potential national policy that would have as its goal the restructuring of the Canadian economy to bring the disparate regions into an integrated economic unit. This would mean investing the revenues from resource extraction into developing the industrial capacity of the hinterland regions, making use of a technology appropriate to the Canadian economy, and ensuring that it is all under the control of Canadian entrepreneurship.

What are the mechanisms through which such a strategy could be initiated? The concept presently used by Alberta and Saskatchewan — of heritage funds in which resource revenues are invested for use in expanding industrial development — seems appropriate. The funds would also be responsible for promoting regionally balanced investment and for developing processes and products which recognize the size and dispersal of the Canadian market. This would not preclude the opening up of new export markets, but, in fact, should encourage exports, with the evolution of new and unique products and capacities.

The second question is where to begin. As a general principle it is advisable to build from strength, and Canada's muscle has been in the resource sector. But while we are one of the world's major producers of raw materials, we are also one of the world's major consumers of imports manufactured from these same raw materials. Alberta, Saskatchewan and Quebec have been moving toward the fostering of industries which convert the natural resources of the hinterland into semi-finished and finished products — whether they be petroleum, asbestos, nickel, paper or food-based products. Nor is this a new direction for Canadian policy: as mentioned earlier, the Ontario and Quebec governments around the turn of the century fostered the development of the pulp and paper industry by restricting the export of unprocessed pulp wood to the United States.

The creative role of the public sector as entrepreneur would make possible the integration of all of these elements, none of which represent any new strategy for Canadian economics. It is a question not of whether it can be done, but rather of whether we have the political will to do it. The possibility exists to integrate the country's regions into a balanced economy where power and wealth are more equally distributed. Failure to do so will inevitably mean continued regional alienation and political disintegration.

Notes on Sources

Chapter 1

The statistics on income per capita, employment, unemployment, population growth and research and development expenditures are taken from the Economic Council of Canada, *Living Together* (Ottawa: Ministry of Supply and Services, 1977). The information for Figure 1-1 is taken from D.M. Ray, "Regional Economic Development and the Location of U.S. Subsidiaries," in Paul Phillips, ed., *Incentives, Location and Regional Development* (Manitoba Economic Development Advisory Board: Winnipeg, 1975), p. 25. The information for Figure 1-2 is taken from Statistics Canada, *Labour Force Information* (71-001), March, 1978. Sylvia Ostry's and Mahmood Zaidi's 1968 study is entitled *Labour Economics in Canada* (Toronto: Macmillan, 1972). The Newfoundland case history is excerpted from Case History #1 in the Report of the People's Commission on Unemployment, published by the Newfoundland and Labrador Federation of Labour. Information on optimal urban population size is from Stuart Holland, *Capital Versus the Regions* (London: Macmillan, 1976).

Chapter 2

The introduction to the section on the Atlantic region is by Joey Smallwood, speaking in 1931. He is quoted by P. Neary and P. O'Flaherty, eds., in *By Great Waters* (Toronto: University of Toronto Press, 1974, pp. 193-4.) The figures for the regional disparity indicators are taken from: Canadian Council on Rural Development, *Regional Poverty and Change*, pp. 151-4, and selected issues of *Canadian Statistical Review*, *Survey of Production: Private and Public Investment in Canada* and *National Accounts: Income and Expenditure*. The figures on sub-regional disparities in Nova Scotia appeared in the Financial Post's *Report on the Nation* (Toronto: Maclean-Hunter, 1977), p. 14. All other references to the *Financial Post* in this section and throughout the book refer to this *Report*. The figures on percentage labour force distribution by industry are from the 1971 *Census of Canada*. The quotation on the problems common to the Maritime provinces is from Richard Caves and Richard Holton, *The Canadian Economy* (Cambridge: Harvard University Press, 1961), p. 145. The quotations in the Quebec section are excerpted from Pierre Fournier, *The Quebec Establishment* (Montreal: Black Rose, 1976). The opening quotation in the Prairies section is from Heather Robertson, *Grass Roots* (Toronto: James Lorimer, 1973). The definition of "agribusiness" is from Don Mitchell, *The Politics of Food* (Toronto: James Lorimer & Co., 1975). The B.C. section is introduced with a quotation from an article by Robert Harlow, "Last Tango in Prince George," in *Macleans* (June 1973), p. 40. The quotation introducing the section on the North is from Phillip Blake's evidence presented to the Berger Royal Commission in *Northern Frontier, Northern Homeland* (Toronto: James Lorimer, 1977). Robert Davis' and Mark Zannis' book is *The Genocide Machine in Canada* (Montreal: Black Rose, 1973). For more information on the Bankslander case, see Peter J. Usher, *The Bankslanders: Economy and Ecol-*

ogy of a Frontier Trapping Community (Ottawa: Information Canada, 1970-71).

Chapter 3

Finance Minister Galt's argument for Confederation is quoted by V.C. Fowke in *The National Policy and the Wheat Economy* (Toronto: University of Toronto Press, 1973), p. 34. The quotation emphasizing the one-way transportation flow from the Maritimes to Central Canada is from W.A. MacIntosh, *The Economic Background of Dominion-Provincial Relations* (Toronto: McClelland and Stewart, 1964), p. 153. The quotation on the western farmers' sacrifice is from V.C. Fowke, "Monetary Policy", *Submission of the Government of Saskatchewan to the Royal Commission on Dominion-Provincial Relations*, Secton C, Part VII (Regina: King's Printer, 1937), p. 25. The statistics on regional concentration of manufacturing production are taken from MacIntosh, p. 97.

Chapter 4

The introductory quotation and other material by Tom Kent (former deputy minister of DREE and now President of Sydney Steel Company) are taken from "The Structure of Canadian Regional Progress", in Phillips, ed., *Incentives, Location and Regional Development*, p. 102. The Rowell-Sirois Commission Report can be found under *Report of the Royal Commission on Dominion-Provincial Relations* (Ottawa, 1940). The figures on DREE expenditure per capita are taken from *Living Together*, p. 152; figures on federal grants and contributions come from the same document, pp. 170, 186. The quotations from DREE are in its 1976 report, *The New Approach* (Ottawa: Ministry of Supply and Services, 1977). Robert Collison's article, "How to Know How Hard the Times Are," appeared in *Saturday Night* (January 1978), p. 26. The quotation from Premier Alex Campbell is taken from "Pioneers of Elegant Frugality," *Saturday Night* (March 1977), p. 31.

Chapter 5

The figures on U.S. imports of resources are taken from Cy Gonick, *Inflation or Depression* (Toronto: James Lorimer, 1975), pp. 241-2, and R.J. Barnet and R.E. Muller, *Global Reach* (N.Y.: Simon and Schuster, 1974), p. 126. The information on the location of multinationals in Canada is from D.M. Ray, "Regional Economic Development." DREE statistics have been taken from *The New Approach*. Michael Bradfield's discussion of DREE can be found in his article, "*Living Together*: A Review," *Canadian Public Policy* (Autumn 1977), p. 504. Dudley and Springate's study of the effects of location grants is in Phillips, ed., *Incentives, Location and Regional Development*. The material on Canadian Research and Development is from *A Science Policy for Canada*, Report of the Special Committee of the Senate on Science Policy, Vol. 4 (1977), p. 10. The Crookell study on the impact of the integration of Canadian and American manufacturing and the figures on Northern Telecom are from A.J. Cordell, *The Multinational Firm: Foreign Direct Investment and Canadian Science Policy* (Ottawa: Science Council of Canada, 1971).

Chapter 6

The quotation on resource rich nations generating their own capital is from Kierans, *Report*, p. 37. The Herschel Hardin quotation is from his book *A Nation Unaware* (Vancouver: J.J. Douglas, 1974), p. 140.

About the Author

Paul Phillips is an associate professor of economics at the University of Manitoba. A former research director for the Manitoba Economic Development Advisory Board, he has published many articles on the problems of the Canadian economy.